Your Space

Student's Book 2

Martyn Hobbs and Julia Starr Keddle

CAMBRIDGE
UNIVERSITY PRESS

CAMBRIDGE UNIVERSITY PRESS
Cambridge, New York, Melbourne, Madrid, Cape Town,
Singapore, São Paulo, Delhi, Mexico City

Cambridge University Press
The Edinburgh Building, Cambridge CB2 8RU, UK

www.cambridge.org
Information on this title: www.cambridge.org/9780521729284

First published 2012
Reprinted 2013

Printed in Italy by L.E.G.O. S.p.A.

A catalogue record for this publication is available from the British Library

ISBN 978-0-521-72928-4 Student's Book, Level 2
ISBN 978-0-521-72929-1 Workbook with Audio CD, Level 2
ISBN 978-0-521-72930-7 Teacher's Book, Level 2
ISBN 978-0-521-72932-1 Class Audio CDs (3), Level 2

Contents

Functions	Skills	
Talking about daily routines	**Reading:** understanding children's descriptions of their best friends **Listening:** understanding children's descriptions of their friends **Speaking:** talking about a friend **Writing:** writing about your best friend	**Pronunciation:** /s/ /z/ /ɪz/ **Study skills:** Scanning
Talking about ability Talking about the present		
Classroom survival		
Talking about the past	**Reading:** understanding a blog about a holiday in Africa **Listening:** understanding a phone conversation about a holiday in Africa **Speaking:** describing your last holiday **Writing:** writing about your last holiday	**Pronunciation:** /t/ /d/ /ɪd/ **Study skills:** Before you listen
Talking about the past		
Asking for information		
Talking about the past	**Reading:** finding out about British legends **Listening:** understanding a radio programme about people's heroes **Speaking:** talking about your hero **Writing:** writing about your hero	**Pronunciation:** /ʃ/ /tʃ/ **Study skills:** Before you read
Asking questions about the past		
Telling a story		
Making comparisons	**Reading:** understanding texts about animals at risk **Listening:** understanding descriptions of animals **Speaking:** talking about the litter problem **Writing:** writing about litter problems where you live	**Pronunciation:** /ɒ/ /əʊ/ **Study skills:** Before you speak
Talking about superlatives		
Shopping		
Talking about future plans	**Reading:** understanding a text about freetime activities **Listening:** completing a text about the Jorvik Viking centre **Speaking:** Talking about activities **Writing:** Writing an email about your weekend	**Pronunciation:** Word stress **Study skills:** Writing an email
Talking about the weekend		
Making arrangements		

Contents

1A That's my life!

Grammar
present simple ® •
some / any ® • countable /
uncountable ® • too much /
too many

Functions
talking about daily routines

Vocabulary • Daily life

1 ◉ **1.02** Listen and repeat the expressions. Then number the activities in the order you do them on a typical school day.

(have breakfast) (get up 1) (go to school) (have lunch) (go to bed) (get washed)

(do my homework) (get dressed) (go home) (have dinner) (watch TV)

2 **Work in pairs. Talk about a typical school day.**

I get up at quarter to seven. I get washed and get dressed.
I usually have cereal and coffee for breakfast.

3 (Circle) five activities that you do. Then try and guess your partner's activities.

play computer games   surf the web   go swimming   play football   collect things
listen to music   meet friends   play a musical instrument   go shopping   read books
play tennis   send text messages   play basketball

A I guess you play computer games.
B You're right!

Presentation

4 **Warm up** Read the penpal exchange on page 9 quickly and underline expressions from the lists in Exercises 1 and 3.

5 ◉ **1.03** Listen and read the penpal exchange. Are the sentences true (*T*) or false (*F*)?

1 Jacob gets up at 6.30 am on a school day. *T*
2 He often plays the drums at home.
3 Kirsty goes to football matches with her sister.
4 Kirsty and Jacob like music.
5 Kirsty watches TV in the afternoon.

6 **Read *Language focus*. Then (circle) examples of the words in bold in the penpal exchange on page 9.**

7 **Tick (✓) the sentences that are true for you. Put a cross (✗) for the sentences that aren't true.**

I've got too many books. ☐
I play too many games. ☐
I've got too much money. ☐
I've got too much free time. ☐
I've got too many clothes. ☐
I eat too much chocolate. ☐

Language focus

• I **usually watch** TV.
• I **often go** to football matches.
• I always have **too much** homework.
• I've got **too many** things.
• I **don't play** a musical instrument.

1.03

Your Space penpal exchange

Penpals

Jacob

Hi Kirsty

I live in Los Angeles with my mom and dad. I usually get up at 6.30 am. That's too early! I go to school by bus. My favorite subject is music. In the afternoon I watch TV or play computer games. But I always have too much homework!

At the weekend I usually hang out with my friends at the skate park. I play baseball and basketball, too. And I sleep a lot!

I play the drums. My mom says, 'You make too much noise!' so I don't often play them at home. But I also love reading.

Sport, music, computers, sleep – that's my life! What do you do in your free time? Have you got any hobbies?

Jacob

Kirsty

Hi Jacob

Thanks for your message. I live in Glasgow with my mum, my stepdad, my brother and sister, and my two cats – Jam and Honey! I love music. But I don't play a musical instrument. My favourite band is Franz Ferdinand (they're from Glasgow!). Do you like them? My favourite subject is sport. I play football in the girls' football team. I'm a Rangers fan and I often go to matches with my family. But my sister doesn't come. She prefers dancing. I collect Rangers souvenirs. I spend too much money on them. And my bedroom is untidy because I've got too many things! I don't like TV. In the evening I listen to music or read a book. Write soon!

Kirsty

Navigation

Home
Penpals
Search
Edit Your Data
Text Chat
FAQs
About Us
Contact Us

Your Space   Talking about your life

8 **Work in pairs. Talk about activities you do:**

reading   your favourite school subject   your favourite music
a sport you play

I play the guitar. I also read lots of books and I love computer games. My favourite school subject is Art. I like Beyoncé. I play football and I go swimming.

9 **Tell the class about your partner's interests.**

My partner plays tennis and football.

(R) Present simple

1 Complete the cartoons with the correct form of the verbs. Use the table to help you.

read   not eat   go

subject	positive	negative
I / you / we / they	eat	don't eat
he / she / it	eat**s**	doesn't eat

questions	short answers
Do they eat?	Yes, they do. No, they don't.
Does she eat?	Yes, she does. No, she doesn't.

We .... to the same school.

Robopet .... dog food.

Zak .... ten books every day.

2 Complete the sentences with the present simple.

1 Pete __wears__ jeans every day! (wear)
2 I .... horror films. (not watch)
3 We .... in town after school. (meet)
4 My sister .... to loud music (listen)
5 Elizabeth .... comics. (collect)
6 My parents .... to work. (not drive)

Soundbite

/s/ /z/ /ɪz/

a ◉ **1.04 Listen and repeat.**
  1 eats   works   sleeps
  2 reads   goes   listens
  3 watches   finishes   loses

b ◉ **1.05 Write the words in the correct columns. Then listen and check.**
  spends   collects   starts   catches   plays
  pushes   likes   wears   washes   surfs
  brushes   cycles   uses   talks   phones

/s/	/z/	/ɪz/

3 ◉ **1.06 Listen to the interview and (circle) Beatriz's answers.**

1 play computer games   (yes) | no
2 like hip-hop music   yes | no
3 play the piano   yes | no
4 watch TV after school   yes | no
5 read lots of books   yes | no
6 go to the beach in the summer yes | no

4 ☆ **Work in pairs. Interview your partner. Use the questions from Exercise 3.**

A Do you play computer games?
B Yes, I do.

5 **Tell the class about your partner.**

Anna plays computer games.

Ⓡ Countable / uncountable

6 **Study these words. Write (C) or (U). Use the table below to help you.**

homework (U)   computer games
noise   music   book   ice cream
souvenir   food   sweets
T-shirt   rain   text message
photo   time   hair   information
paper   idea   money

There are	**some**	sweets on my desk.
Julie has got	**some**	cool music on her mp3 player.
I haven't got	**any**	new books.
Is there	**any**	interesting information on that website?

7 🔘 **1.07** **What's on the school website? Listen and tick (✓) or cross (✗) the student's notes.**

THE NEW SCHOOL WEBSITE

photos   music
blogs   games
a magazine   homework
films   information
stories

8 🖉 **Write sentences about the school website.**

There are some ...
There aren't any ...

9 ☆ **Work in pairs. Ask and answer questions about the website.**

A Are there any photos on the website?
B Yes, there are. There are lots of photos of students and teachers.

too much / too many

10 **Complete the sentences with *much* or *many*.**

1 I eat too ...many... sweets.
2 I've got too .... clothes.
3 I watch too .... TV.
4 I send too .... text messages.
5 I've got too .... books in my bag.
6 I spend too .... time on the internet.

11 ☆ **Work in pairs. Tick the sentences in Exercise 10 which are true for you. Tell your partner.**

Grammar

present continuous Ⓡ • present simple / present continuous • can Ⓡ • very / really / quite Ⓡ

Functions

talking about ability • talking about the present

Vocabulary • Jobs in the house

1 🔘 **1.08 Match the jobs with the pictures. Then listen and check.**

lay the table ☐   tidy your room 1   put out the rubbish ☐   walk the dog ☐

clear the table ☐   make breakfast ☐   wash the dishes ☐   make your bed ☐

2 Work in pairs. Which jobs do you do? Tell your partner.

I always tidy my room. I never clear the table!

Presentation

3 Warm up Look at the photos on page 13 and answer the questions.

Who can you see? Where are they? What are Harry and Jack doing?

4 🔘 **1.09 Listen and read the photo story. Then answer the questions.**

1 What are Jack and Harry doing?

2 What do they want to send to Africa?

3 Who is paying them to clean cars?

4 What does Alice usually do after school?

5 What does Harry always do after school?

6 Who joins Jack's Africa Challenge team?

5 Read Language focus. Then complete the conversations with the correct form of the verb.

1 A What time .... (you / get up)?

  B I usually .... (get up) at quarter to six.

2 A What .... (Lucy / do) at the moment?

  B She .... (write) an email.

6 🔘 **1.10 Listen and write what Dylan is doing.**

1 He's making his bed.

Language focus

• Jack and Harry **aren't going** home.

• They **are working**.

• **Are** you **doing** the Africa Challenge?

• I usually **go** home and **do** my homework, but today **I'm cleaning** cars!

• I'm **really** tired.

• I'm **quite** fast.

A 1.09 It's the end of the school day. But at the moment Jack and Harry aren't hanging out together. They're working!

Poppy Hi guys! What are you doing?
Jack We're cleaning cars! I'm washing the outside of the car.
Harry And I'm cleaning the inside!
Poppy Why are you doing that? Are you in trouble?
Jack No, we aren't! This is for a class project. It's the Africa Challenge!
Harry We want to send computers to schools in Africa.
Poppy That's a brilliant idea. But how does this help?
Jack Because we're collecting money for charity. The teachers and parents are paying us!

B Alice is helping too.

Alice Come on, Harry. There are three more cars to clean!
Poppy Are you doing the Africa Challenge too?
Alice Yes, I am. I usually go home and do my homework in the afternoon. But today I'm cleaning cars!
Harry And I always sleep after school! I'm really tired now.

C Poppy has an idea.

Poppy Can I help, Jack?
Jack Yes, of course. Can you wash cars?
Poppy Yes, I can. I clean my mum's car. I'm quite fast.
Jack Poppy, you're in our Africa Challenge team!

Your Space Talking about the present

7 Imagine you are in one of these places. What are you doing?

park   fast-food restaurant   sports centre   shop   cinema
train station   museum

sports centre – playing volleyball

8 Work in pairs. Act out telephone conversations.

A Hi. Where are you?   **B** I'm in a sports centre.
A What are you doing?   **B** I'm playing volleyball.

Chat zone
Are you in trouble?
That's a brilliant idea.
Come on.

Present continuous

1 **Complete the sentences with the verbs in brackets.**

1 Max _is listening_ (listen) to music. He _isn't doing_ (not do) his homework.

2 Robopet .... (sleep). He .... (not play) a video game.

3 Lara .... (not watch) TV. She .... (talk) on her mobile.

4 Dad and Zak .... (watch) TV. They .... (not read).

5 Mum and Grandad .... (not sit) on the sofa. They .... (drink) coffee at the table.

2 ✿ **Work in pairs. Ask and answer questions about the picture.**

A Is Grandad dancing?
B No, he isn't.
A Is he wearing a hat?
B Yes, he is.

Get it right!

Be careful to spell the *-ing* form of the verb correctly:

going NOT ~~goin~~
shopping NOT ~~shoping~~

Present simple / present continuous

3 ◉ **1.11** **Alice is on a school trip. Listen and write *U* (usually) or *T* (today).**

My camping trip in The Lake District by Alice
We're camping this weekend. It's all different!

1

2

3

4

5

4 ✎ **Write sentences about Alice.**

1 sleep in her bedroom / sleep in a tent
Alice usually sleeps in her bedroom. Today she's sleeping in a tent.

2 go shopping on Saturdays / make a fire

3 wear school uniform on Mondays / wear jeans

4 have sandwiches for lunch / have sausages

5 watch TV in the evening / have a party

can

5 ✏ **Write sentences or questions with can or can't.**

1 my mum / play the piano ✓
My mum can play the piano.
2 we / help you find it **?**
3 you / write emails in English ✓
4 she / juggle three balls ✗
5 he / draw **?**

6 ☆ **Work in pairs. Ask and answer questions.**

cook	ride a bike	do karate

swim 100 metres	stand on your head

speak another language

A Can you cook?
B Yes, I can. / No, I can't.

very / really / quite

7 **Do the questionnaire. Circle the best answers for you.**

1 How are you today?
not very well | quite well | very well

2 How fast can you run?
not very fast | quite fast | very fast

3 What do you think of Avatar?
not very good | quite good | really good

4 How easy is this exercise?
not very easy | quite easy | very easy

5 What do you think of salad?
not very nice | quite nice | really nice

6 How well can you speak English?
not very well | quite well | very well

8 ☆ **Work in pairs. Ask and answer the questions.**

A How are you today?
B I'm not very well.

➤ **Language check page 128**

Multi-word verbs

Many verbs in English have two parts: verb + preposition or adverb. The original meaning of the verb often changes.

Olivia **wakes up** at half past six.

She usually **gets up** at quarter to seven.

She **puts on** her jumper.

When the teacher arrives, the students **stand up**.

The teacher says, '**Sit down**, class.'

When she gets home, she **takes off** her school jacket.

Olivia and her friends often **hang out** in the park in the afternoon.

9 ☆ **Work in pairs. Ask and answer.**

1 How do you wake up? Do you use an alarm clock?
2 What time do you get up on Mondays?
3 On a school day what clothes do you put on?
4 Does your class stand up when the teacher arrives?
5 Where do you hang out with your friends?

1C Skills

Vocabulary • Describing people

1 **1.13** **Match the anagrams with the words in the box. Then listen and check.**

| honest | shy | friendly | ~~cheerful~~ | generous | lazy | loyal | ~~funny~~ |

1 Lucy tells a lot of jokes and makes people laugh. N Y U F N *funny*
2 Robert always smiles and laughs. L E R E F H U C *cheerful*
3 Emily always tells the truth. S E N T O H
4 Samuel shares his things. S R E U N E O G
5 Lily talks to new students at school. E D I N R F L Y
6 Rebecca hates doing her homework. Z Y A L
7 Jonathan doesn't like parties. H Y S
8 Olivia never says bad things about her friends. A L Y L O

2 **Work in pairs and complete the spidergrams.**

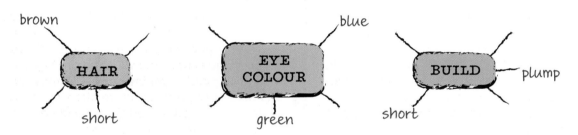

DESCRIBING PEOPLE

brown — HAIR — short

blue — EYE COLOUR — green

BUILD — plump / short

3 **1.14** **Listen to Lee's descriptions of his friends and number the pictures in the order you hear them.**

4 **1.14** **Listen again and make notes about the personality of each person.**

1 *cheerful, funny*

Reading and listening

5 ⊙ **1.15** **Read and listen to the web page. Are the sentences true (*T*) or false (*F*)?**

1 Madison and Samantha sit together in school. *T*
2 Samantha helps Madison with her homework.
3 Madison and Samantha both love sport.
4 Simon and Joe go to the same school.
5 Simon likes playing computer games.
6 Simon and Joe never disagree.

| Home | Contact | Help | Log in |

What's your best friend like?

My best friend's name is Madison. She's 13. We're in the same class, and we always sit together. She's good at Maths and helps me with my homework. She's got long fair hair and green eyes. Madison is quite tall, and she's got a lovely smile. She's very generous, and I can tell her all my problems. We both love shopping and sport... and fast food! **Samantha**

My best friend is Simon. He's 12. He's got short dark hair, and he's quite short. He's got a cheeky smile and he's really funny. I love his jokes! We don't go to the same school, but we hang out together at the weekends. We've got the same interests. We both like computer games, and we often listen to music on the same mp3 player! Simon and I only argue about one thing – football! **Joe**

What makes a good friend?

A good friend is honest and loyal. You can trust her. *Skye, 13*

You share your secrets. She helps you when you've got a problem. *Abby, 12*

A good friend listens to you. And he has the same interests. *Ross, 12*

A good friend remembers your birthday! She's cheerful and makes you smile. *Beth, 13*

A good friend likes you. He doesn't try to change you. *Brandon, 12*

Speaking and writing

6 **Complete the sentences with your own ideas.**

A good friend is ...   A good friend doesn't ...   A good friend ...   You can ... with a good friend.

7 **Work in pairs. Describe your best friend. Talk about:**

• age   • appearance   • personality   • things you do together

8 **Write a description of your best friend. Use the information in Exercise 7.**

Communication page 108   Your Space Web Zone   (People   Unit 1   **17**)

Grammar
past simple *be*: all forms Ⓡ •
there was / there were

Functions
talking about the past

Vocabulary • Transport

1 🔊 **1.18** **Match the words with the pictures. Then listen and check.**

car ☐   ship ☐   plane ☐   motorbike ☐   bus ☐ 1

train ☐   helicopter ☐   bicycle (bike) ☐   boat ☐   lorry ☐

2 **Complete the spidergrams with the words from Exercise 1.**

ship

WATER

LAND

AIR

Presentation

3 **Warm up** **Read about the bike ride on page 19 and answer the questions.**

1 What day is the bike ride?
2 What time does the ride start?
3 How long is the ride?
4 Why are they doing the sponsored ride?

4 🔊 **1.19** **Listen and read the photo story on page 19. Then write the names.**

1 Alice has got lots of sponsors.
2 … isn't in the park.
3 … makes a phone call.
4 … is fast.
5 … has got a problem with his mobile phone.
6 … has got a problem with his bike.

5 **Read *Language focus*. Then find four more sentences in the past in the photo story.**

6 🔊 **1.20** **Complete Poppy's email with *was*, *were* or *wasn't*. Listen and check.**

Hi Amy!
The bike ride **1**............... fantastic! There **2**...............
lots of students. We **3**............... all in the park at
nine o'clock. Unfortunately, Harry **4**............... in the
park with us. He **5**............... ill, but there **6**...............
a problem with his bike. The ride **7**............... ten
kilometres long. I **8**............... very tired!
See you tomorrow.
Poppy

Language focus

• I **was** with Harry yesterday.
• You **were** really fast.
• He **wasn't** ill.
• Where **were** you at
  10 o'clock?

SPONSORED BIKE RIDE

Sunday, 18 May at 10 am
From Cambridge to Grantchester and back.
Please sponsor our 10 km ride.
Help us to send computers to schools in Africa.

A 🔘 **1.19 Jack, Poppy and Alice and their classmates are ready for their sponsored bike ride. But where's Harry?**

Poppy	How many sponsors have you got, Alice?
Alice	I've got loads. My parents, my uncles and aunts …
Poppy	Harry's really late. Do you think he's ill?
Jack	I was with Harry yesterday. We were at the skate park. He wasn't ill!
Poppy	I can call him … Where are you, Harry? Call us!
Teacher	Come on, you three! It's time to start.
Jack	OK, let's go! Without Harry!

B **After the ride…**

Alice	Wow! That was fantastic!
Poppy	You were really fast, Alice.
Alice	Thanks. But you two weren't slow!

C **Ten minutes later they see Harry!**

Harry	This morning was a disaster!
Poppy	Was there a problem with your mobile phone?
Harry	Yes, there was. The battery was flat.
Alice	Was there a lot of traffic?
Harry	No, there wasn't.
Jack	So where were you at ten o'clock? What was the problem?
Harry	Look at my bike! Two flat tyres!
Poppy	Poor Harry! That's so unlucky!

Your Space Talking about the past

7 **Think about when you were eight years old, and answer the questions.**

Who was your best friend?   My best friend was Bulent.
What was your favourite food?
Where was your school?
Who was your favourite singer or band?
What was your favourite TV programme?

8 **Work in pairs. Compare your sentences.**

Chat zone

I've got loads.
This morning was a disaster.
That's so unlucky!

Ⓡ **Past simple be**

1 **Look at the table and complete the cartoons.**

subject	positive	negative
I / he / she / it	was	wasn't
we / you / they	were	weren't
questions		
Was	I / he / she / it ... ?	
Were	we / you / they ... ?	

short answers		
Yes,	I / he / she / it	was.
	we / you / they	were.
No,	I / he / she / it	wasn't.
	we / you / they	weren't.

Zak .... at home yesterday.

He .... at the doctor's. And he .... very happy!

2 **Complete the blogs with was / wasn't / were / weren't.**

My terrible day!

I ¹............ (✔) at school yesterday and it ²............ (✔) terrible! My homework ³............ (✗) in my bag. It ⁴............ (✔) on my desk in my bedroom! And my teacher ⁵............ (✔) very annoyed! Tell me about your terrible day!

Dan

My parents ⁶............ (✗) happy with me. First I ⁷............ (✔) late for school. Then my room ⁸............ (✔) a mess. And finally my friends ⁹............ (✔) very noisy in the afternoon.

JoJo

Lots of people ¹⁰............ (✔) annoyed with me yesterday evening. We ¹¹............ (✔) in the cinema and it ¹²............ (✔) a very sad film. Then there ¹³............ (✔) a call on my mobile phone. It ¹⁴............ (✔) very loud!

Alicia

3 📖 **Read the blogs. Are the sentences true (T) or false (F)?**

1 Dan's homework was in his bag.
2 His teacher was annoyed with him.
3 JoJo's parents were happy.
4 Her friends were very quiet.
5 There was a funny film on at the cinema.
6 Alicia's mobile phone was very loud.

4 ✍ **Write the questions.**

1 your parents / at home / last night?
Were your parents at home last night?
2 your best friend / sad / yesterday?
3 you / tired / on Monday morning?
4 Maths lesson / last week / easy?
5 your favourite programme / on TV last night?
6 you in the park / yesterday?

5 ☆ **Work in pairs. Ask and answer the questions.**

A Were your parents at home last night?
B Yes, they were.

there was / there were

6 Circle the correct words. Use the table to help you.

1 There *was* / *were* some problems with my computer.
2 There *was* / *were* lots of flowers on our balcony this summer.
3 There *was* / *were* some good news in our History lesson. No homework!
4 There *was* / *were* fantastic special effects in that film.
5 There *was* / *were* lots of nice people at the party.
6 There *was* / *were* a new email in my inbox.

positive	negative
There was …	There wasn't …
There were …	There weren't …
questions	**short answers**
Was there … ?	Yes, there was. No, there wasn't.
Were there … ?	Yes, there were. No, there weren't.

7 Complete the conversation with the correct form of *there was / there were*.

Keira ¹ There was a fantastic party at Holly's house on Saturday. Look at this photo.

Jason Wow! ² _____ lots of people!

Keira Yes, ³ _____ lots of Holly's friends. And her parents were there, too. But ⁴ _____ any other adults.

Jason ⁵ _____ any music?

Keira Yes, ⁶ _____ and it was really loud!

Jason ⁷ _____ lots of food to eat?

Keira Yes, ⁸ _____ . _____ sandwiches and bowls of crisps.

Jason ⁹ _____ a big birthday cake?

Keira No, ¹⁰ _____ . Holly doesn't like cake, but ¹¹ _____ a big pizza. And ¹² _____ candles in it!

8 1.21 Check your answers. Then act out the conversation.

9 Work in pairs. Cover the picture. Ask and answer questions.

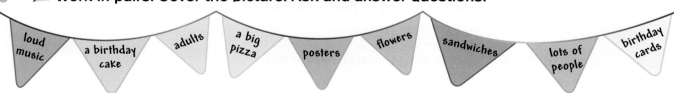

loud music | a birthday cake | adults | a big pizza | posters | flowers | sandwiches | lots of people | birthday cards

A Was there a big pizza at the party?
B Yes, there was.

2B And then we waited...

Grammar
past simple: positive • prepositions of time • regular and irregular verbs

Functions
talking about the past

Vocabulary • Airport

1 🔘 **1.22** **Match the words with the pictures. Then listen and check.**

gate ☐   passport control ☐   pilot ☐   check-in ☐
plane ☐1   baggage reclaim ☐   flight attendant ☐   runway ☐

2 **Answer the questions. Where do you ...?**

- leave your luggage
- collect your luggage
- show your passport

Presentation

3 **Warm up Look at the pictures on page 23.**

What do you think the email is about?

4 🔘 **1.23** **Listen and read the email. Then number the pictures in order.**

5 **Read Sam's email again and match the times with the actions.**

1	3 pm	**a**	they went through passport control
2	6 pm	**b**	they found a hotel
3	8 pm	**c**	they had bad news
4	10 pm	**d**	they left the hotel
5	12 am	**e**	they arrived at Heathrow Airport
6	9 am	**f**	they arrived at Pisa Airport

6 **Read *Language focus*. Then match the past simple with these verbs.**

eat *ate* cry go stay have play

7 **Underline the past simple forms of these verbs in Sam's email.**

leave arrive see wait find listen

8 **Complete the sentences about yesterday for you.**

1 I went to school by bike yesterday.
2 I studied ....
3 I watched ....
4 I ate ....
5 I listened to ....
6 I went to bed at ....

Language focus

- I **played** football with some Italian boys.
- My sister **watched** cartoons.
- We **stayed** in a cool hotel.
- Ruby **cried**.
- I **ate** ice cream.
- We **had** a flight at 7.30 am.
- We **went** to Italy.

email
of the week

My last summer holiday was fantastic. There was only one problem – the journey home!

We went to Italy three months ago (that's me, my mum and dad, and my four-year-old sister Ruby). We stayed in a cool hotel near the sea. I went swimming every day and played football with some Italian boys on the beach. I also ate great pizzas and ice cream!

After two amazing weeks, it was time to go home. We left the hotel at 3 pm and went to Pisa Airport by coach. The hotel was only 25 kilometres from the airport and our flight was at 7 pm, so we had lots of time. But there was a terrible traffic jam on the motorway and we arrived at the airport at 6 pm!

We saw big queues at the check-in. There was a problem with the computers! Fortunately, our plane was late. Its new departure time was 9.15 pm.

We went through passport control at 8 pm.

And then we waited... and waited. Ruby was hungry and thirsty, and she cried a lot. At 10 pm, we had bad news. Our flight was cancelled.

We found a hotel near the airport at midnight. We had a flight at 7.30 am. So the next morning we were very tired. My sister Ruby cried again!

Ruby watched cartoons on the plane and I listened to my mp3 player. We arrived at Heathrow Airport at 9 o'clock in the morning! And then, guess what? Our suitcases weren't at baggage reclaim. They were still in Italy!

By Sam

Your Space Talking about the past

9 **Work in groups. Say what you did on Saturday. Use the verbs to help you.**

did visited saw watched played went on the internet listened

A I did my homework on Saturday. And I visited my grandparents.
B I went on the internet.
C Me too! And I played football in the park with my friends.

Past simple – regular verbs

1 **Read and complete Jasmine's diary with the correct form of the verb in brackets.**

I / you / he / she / it / we / they	listen**ed**

Diary

Monday
I ¹_____ (text) my friend Jenna in America yesterday.

Tuesday
We ²_____ (visit) the Science Museum. Cool!

Wednesday
We ³_____ (watch) a boring film last night. ☹

Thursday
My sister Jessica ⁴_____ (arrive) late for work today.

Friday
Jessica ⁵_____ (decide) to get up early this morning! ☺

Saturday
I ⁶_____ (practise) the piano in the morning.

Sunday
David and I ⁷_____ (walk) for three hours in the countryside. Very tiring! My dad ⁸_____ (cook) a roast dinner.

Soundbite

/t/ /d/ /ɪd/

a ◉ **1.24** **Listen and repeat.**
1 talked   finished
2 arrived   played
3 started   decided

b ◉ **1.25** **Listen to the verbs. Are they 1, 2 or 3?**

sailed [2]   watched [ ]   travelled [ ]
visited [ ]   followed [ ]   worked [ ]
lived [ ]   cooked [ ]   invited [ ]

Past simple – irregular verbs

2 ◉ **1.26** **Match the verbs with their past forms. Then listen and check.**

do   win   come   write   give   wear   know   lose   ride

rode   gave   knew   wrote   won   did   lost   came   wore

3 **Complete the sentences with the verbs from Exercise 2.**

1 Marek _wrote_ an email to his American friend Josh last night.
2 Our dad _____ a terrible hat to the school open day.
3 Omar and Khaled _____ on an elephant at the safari park.
4 Mum _____ me a new bike. I love it.
5 Poor Sophie! She _____ her mobile phone in the shopping centre.
6 Jo _____ a prize in the art contest.

4 ◉ **1.27** **Listen and circle the correct words.**

Jamie's day

		a	b
1	get up	(7.15 am)	7.45 am
2	have breakfast	a cereal	b toast and jam
3	leave home	a 8.15 am	b 8.45 am
4	eat	a chicken	b sandwiches
5	lose	a keys	b mobile phone
6	send	a text messages	b emails
7	read	a book	b comic
8	go to bed	a 10.20 pm	b 10.30 pm

5 ✎ **Write sentences about Jamie.**

Jamie got up at quarter past seven.

6 ◉ **1.28** Complete the review with the past simple. Then listen and check.

Holiday reviews

| **Egypt** | Japan | Mexico |

Last December we **1**_____ (go) to Egypt. We **2**_____ (fly) to Cairo. On the first morning we **3**_____ (ride) on camels. Then we **4**_____ (climb) up the Pyramids. One day we **5**_____ (drive) into the desert. I **6**_____ (love) it. The next day we **7**_____ (sail) on a boat up the River Nile. I **8**_____ (swim) in the Red Sea and **9**_____ (see) some incredible fish. One evening a local family **10**_____ (cook) us a meal – we **11**_____ (eat) very well. I really **12**_____ (enjoy) the holiday, but I was happy to get back and see my friends.

7 **Write sentences about your last holiday.**

I went to Paris.

8 **Work in groups. Talk about your holidays.**

A I went to China last year and I visited The Great Wall.
B I stayed with my aunt in Paris.
C Cool! I climbed a mountain in Scotland.

> **Language check page 128**

Talking about time

at • time

at seven o'clock   **at** night

in • parts of the day

in the morning **in** the afternoon **in** the evening

• months, seasons, years

in summer   **in** 1969
in winter   **in** June

on • dates

on 21 February   **on** 1 January

9 **Complete the sentences with the correct prepositions.**

1 My birthday is _on_____ 21st September.
2 See you _____ half past six!
3 It's often hot and sunny _____ the summer.
4 I usually do my homework _____ the afternoon, but sometimes I do it _____ night!
5 There's a football world cup _____ 2018.

Vocabulary • Animals

1 🔊 **1.30** **Match the words with the pictures. Then listen and check.**

leopard ☐ ostrich ☐ lion ☐ giraffe ☐ flamingo ☐
rhinoceros (rhino) [1] zebra ☐ snake ☐ elephant ☐
hippopotamus (hippo) ☐ cheetah ☐ antelope ☐

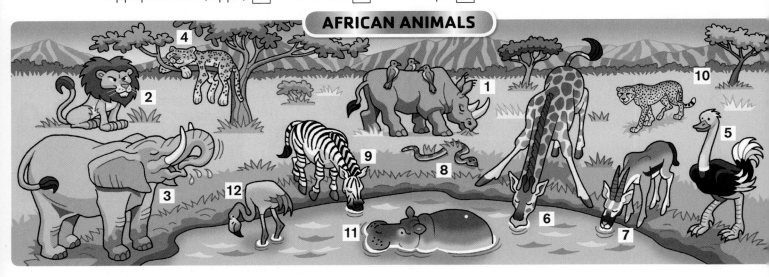

AFRICAN ANIMALS

Reading and listening

2 **Read the blog on page 27 and write the names of the animals Jessica saw.**

3 **Read the blog again and put these sentences in order.**

They had a barbecue.

They got up very early.

They saw elephants.

Jessica bought souvenirs at a market.

They went on a walking safari.

They met some lions.

Adam met them at the airport. 1

They swam in the swimming pool.

Jessica slept badly.

They saw hippos in the river.

4 🔊 **1.31** **Listen to Jessica talking to her friend Tom. Are the sentences true (T) or false (F)?**
1 Jessica and her parents got up at six o'clock. F
2 Jessica went swimming in the morning.
3 Jessica wrote postcards in the afternoon.
4 Her parents went to a market in the afternoon.
5 In the first five hours, they saw two giraffes and a lion.
6 The leopards swam across the river.
7 Jessica took a photo of the leopards.
8 Jessica went to bed after 12 o'clock.

Study skills

Before you listen
Questions help you predict. Look at Exercise 4. What form are the verbs? What is the topic? What vocabulary do you expect to hear?

http://yourspace.cambridge.org

Home   Blog   About Us   Contact

African safari

My holiday blog by Jessica

Day 1

The flight to Zambia took 16 hours! Our guide, Adam, drove us to the camp from the airport. The jeep was very uncomfortable, but finally we got to the camp. We sat by the river and saw lots of hippos. Then we ate cake and drank tea. At four o'clock we went for a drive. We saw zebras and giraffes. Cool! On our way back to the camp, we met some lions. Lucky we were in the jeep!

Day 2

The first night in the chalet was very noisy! I'm sure I heard lions. I had a bad night, but Mum and Dad slept all night. We got up at 5 am for a morning drive. We saw a family of elephants. Awesome! In the afternoon we went to a market and bought souvenirs.

Day 3

This morning we went on a walking safari. A rhinoceros ran towards us. Scary! We took lots of photos. After the walk we swam in the swimming pool. In the evening Adam made a fire and we had a barbecue. There weren't any leopards today. Maybe tomorrow.

Speaking and writing

5   Write notes about your last holiday. Tell your partner about it.
Then write an account.

I went with my family / my school, etc.
We went to the beach / the mountains / London, etc.
We went by car / train / plane, etc.
We stayed in a hotel / in a tent / in a holiday apartment, etc.
I saw ...
We swam / went sailing / visited museums / played football, etc.
We bought ...
We stayed for four days / a week / ten days, etc.

Vocabulary • Disasters

1 ○ **1.34 Match the words with the pictures. Then listen and check.**

hurricane ☐   earthquake ☐   flood ☐   car crash ☐

explosion ☐   drowning ☐   fire ☐

Presentation

2 **Warm up Look at the pictures on page 29.**

What do you think the stories are about?

3 ○ **1.35 Listen and read the web page. Decide if the sentences are true (*T*), false (*F*) or it doesn't say (*DS*).**

1 Blake saw the swimmers in the sea. T

2 He wasn't scared of the high waves.

3 He knew the swimmers.

4 Sammy woke up Mrs King with her paw.

5 Mr and Mrs King took their daughters outside.

6 Mr King went back into the house to save the pets.

4 **Read *Language focus* and underline one more example with *didn't* on the web page.**

5 **Complete the sentences with the names.**

Blake (x2)   Mr King   The Kings (x2)

1 _Blake_ .... wasn't afraid.

2 .... didn't hear the fire.

3 .... didn't stop there.

4 .... didn't forget Sammy.

5 .... didn't smell the smoke.

Language focus

• He **didn't stop** there.
• He **didn't forget** Sammy.
• They **didn't smell** the smoke.

○ 1.35

Life-savers!

Teen hero saved two people

Blake White is only thirteen years old, but he's a hero! Blake is a life-saver with the Golden Bay Life-Saving Club in Fremantle, Australia.

One afternoon, Blake saw a group of adult swimmers in danger. The waves were over two metres high, but he wasn't afraid. He took a surfboard and jumped into the sea. He brought one of the swimmers back to the beach.

And Blake didn't stop there. He went back and rescued another person!

Dog saved four people, two cats and a parrot

Haley King is thirteen years old and her dog Sammy is thirteen, too.

Sammy has only got three legs. But she is a life-saver! On a cold night in February, a fire broke out in the Kings' house. Sammy's family didn't hear the fire and they didn't smell the smoke. But Haley's mum woke up when she felt the dog's paw on her face.

Haley's parents woke up Haley and her brother, Tom, and quickly took them outside. Then her dad went back into the house and rescued their two cats and their parrot. And he didn't forget Sammy, of course!

Your Space   Talking about the past

6   **Write six sentences about things you didn't do yesterday (five true sentences and one false sentence).**

I didn't eat any chocolate. I didn't send text messages to my friends.

7   **Work in pairs. Read your sentences to each other. Can you guess the false sentence?**

Past simple – negative

1 Complete the sentences with the verbs in the table.

I / you he / she / it we / they	did not (didn't)	go win have

Why were Max, Lara, Zak and Robopet unhappy yesterday?

1

Zak _____ a game of chess.

2

Robopet _____ breakfast.

3

Max and Lara _____ to the beach.

2 Complete the sentences with the negative form of the verbs.

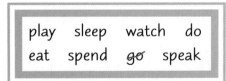

play   sleep   watch   do
eat   spend   ~~go~~   speak

1 I got the bus to school with Emily this morning, but I _didn't go_ home with her in the afternoon.
2 We bought lots of things, but we _____ much money.
3 James stayed at home last night, but he _____ TV.
4 My friend phoned me from Canada but she _____ for long.
5 They met outside the park, but they _____ football there.
6 We went to a Spanish restaurant last night, but we _____ paella.
7 The teacher was annoyed because I _____ my homework.
8 Emma's really tired because she _____ very well last night.

3 ⭐ **Work in pairs. Write five things you think your partner did not do at the weekend. Say your sentences.**

A You didn't eat fish.
B That's false. I had fish on Saturday.

B You didn't speak Chinese.
A That's true.

Get it right!

I **didn't like** the film.   NOT   ~~I didn't liked the film.~~
They **weren't** tired.   NOT   ~~They didn't be tired.~~

4 Write the sentences in the negative.

1 I ate an ice cream yesterday.
  I didn't eat an ice cream yesterday.
2 Olivia listened to the radio before school.
3 We arrived late for school on Monday.
4 You sang really well this morning.
5 Ellie was at the party last night.
6 Andrew forgot his homework yesterday.
7 They drove to the mountains last week.
8 He left his school bag on the bus.

5 **Complete the article with the correct form of the verbs in brackets.**

MY REPORT by Nicky Ellis
ECO heroes for a day!

Rubbish on the beach is bad for people and animals. So last Friday we ¹ _didn't have_ (not have) lessons at school, we ² .... (have) a beach clean-up day. We ³ .... (collect) lots of plastic things. We also ⁴ .... (find) some very big rubbish – washing machines, fridges and tyres, but we ⁵ .... (not collect) that. And we ⁶ .... (not touch) broken glass because it's dangerous. At 12.30 pm we ⁷ .... (stop) for lunch and ⁸ .... (play) beach volleyball. My team ⁹ .... (not win). We ¹⁰ .... (not go) swimming because it was too cold. After lunch we ¹¹ .... (put) our rubbish from lunch in bags – we ¹² .... (not leave) it on the beach, of course! It was a fantastic day. We ¹³ .... (see) two dolphins. But we ¹⁴ .... (not see) any sharks! At the end of the day we had 15 bags of rubbish.

6 **Read the article again. Are the sentences true (T) or false (F)?**

1 Nicky didn't have lessons at school on Friday. T
2 Nicky didn't collect lots of plastic things.
3 Nicky's team didn't win the game of volleyball.
4 Nicky didn't stop for lunch.
5 Nicky didn't go swimming.
6 Nicky didn't see any dolphins.

could

7 **What could Charles do when he was eight years old? Put a tick (✓) or a cross (✗).**

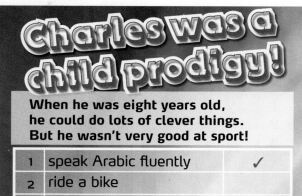

When he was eight years old, he could do lots of clever things. But he wasn't very good at sport!

1	speak Arabic fluently	✓
2	ride a bike	
3	swim	
4	program the computer	
5	play tennis	
6	catch a ball	
7	beat his father at chess	
8	draw very well	

8 **Write sentences about Charles with could/couldn't.**

Charles could speak Arabic fluently when he was eight.

9 **Work in pairs. Ask your partner questions from Exercise 7.**

A Could you swim when you were eight?
B Yes, I could.

Soundbite

/ʃ/ /tʃ/

a **1.36** **Listen and repeat.**
Charlie's always cheerful,
Shannon's sometimes shy,
Charlie's got a cheeky smile,
He's a very funny guy!
Shannon often goes shopping,
Charlie watches TV,
He chats with Shannon on his mobile,
When she chooses DVDs!

b **1.36** **Listen again and circle the /ʃ/ sounds and underline the /tʃ/ sounds.**

3B What did you do?

Grammar
past simple: questions, short
answers and question words

Functions
asking questions about
the past

Vocabulary • Feelings

1 🔘 **1.37** Match the anagrams with the words in the box. Listen and check.
Then match the pictures with the sentences.

annoyed   bored   excited   worried   ~~upset~~   embarrassed   scared

1 Holly felt **T S P U E**. Her friend didn't ask her to her party.   *upset*
2 There was nothing good on TV last night. Holly was very **E R D B O**.
3 Holly was **N A D O N E Y** because her brother broke her mobile phone.

4 She felt **D E C T I E X** when she bought tickets for the Leona Lewis concert! `1`
5 After she read a horror story she was very **R A C D E S**.
6 Holly was very **D R E W O I R**. She had a difficult Maths test.
7 She fell over in the street. She was very **D R E S A S A R B E M**.

Presentation

2 **Warm up** Who can you see in the photos on page 33? Where are they?

3 🔘 **1.38** Listen and read the photo story. Then answer the questions.
1 Who is Miss Evans?   *Their teacher*
2 Where were the team on Friday?
3 What was the problem with the cakes?
4 How does Poppy feel? Why?
5 How does Jack feel? Why?
6 Who has got an idea?

4 Read *Language focus*. Then find all the questions in the story. What are the answers?

5 Write your own answers to the questions below.
What time did you get up this morning?
How many text messages did you send yesterday?
What did you have for breakfast?
Where did you go at the weekend?
What time did you go to bed last night?
How did you come to school today?

6 Work with a partner. Ask and answer the questions.
A What time did you get up?
B At ten past seven.

Language focus
- **Did** you **have** a good week?
- **Yes**, we **did**.
- **Did** they **taste** nice?
- **No**, they **didn't**.
- **What did** you **do**?
- **Where did** you **make** them?

A 🔘 1.38 **The team talk about the Africa Challenge project with their teacher.**

Miss Evans	Did you have a good week?
Alice	Yes, we did. Well … it was OK.
Miss Evans	What did you do?
Jack	Well, last Monday we cleaned cars after school. That was good.
Poppy	Then on Friday we made cakes.
Miss Evans	Where did you make them?
Poppy	At Harry's place.
Miss Evans	Did they taste nice?
Jack	No, they didn't.
Miss Evans	Oh dear!
Harry	Jack put in too much sugar! So we couldn't sell them.
Jack	Hey, it wasn't my fault! I couldn't find the recipe!
Miss Evans	Did you go on the sponsored bike ride?
Poppy	Yes, we did. We raised £80.
Alice	But Harry couldn't do it.
Harry	My bike had two flat tyres! I was really annoyed!
Poppy	We're a bit fed up, Miss. We need some new ideas.
Miss Evans	Well, hurry up, guys! You haven't got a lot of time.

B **The team must think of new ideas to raise money. And fast!**

Alice	What's up, Jack?
Jack	I'm really worried. I want our team to win the Challenge. But what can we do next?
Alice	I don't know.
Poppy	Have you got any ideas, Harry?
Harry	Yes, I have actually. Listen …

Your Space Asking about yesterday

7 **Work in pairs. Ask and answer questions about yesterday. Try to give more information.**

Did you … watch TV / do any homework / send an email / surf the web / eat a banana / drink any fruit juice / do a sport / see your friends?

A Did you watch TV yesterday?
B No, I didn't. / Yes, I did. I watched a quiz show.

8 **Ask your own questions.**

Chat zone
at Harry's place
Oh dear!
It wasn't my fault!
a bit fed up
What's up?

Past simple – questions, short answers and question words

	Did you have fun?	Yes, we did.
	Did they taste nice?	No, they didn't.
What	did you do?	We …
Where	did you go?	We went …

1 🔘 **1.39** Listen to Jacob and Lauren talking about their weekend. What did they do? Tick (✓) or cross (✗).

Last weekend...

	Jacob	Lauren
go swimming		
see friends		
help your parents		
visit relatives		
get up late		
do any homework		

2 ☆ Work in pairs. Ask questions about Jacob and Lauren.

A Did Jacob go swimming?
B Yes, he did.

3 ☆ Ask and answer questions about last weekend.

A Did you go swimming?
B No, I didn't.

4 **Read and complete the interview with the question words below.**

when who what where why how

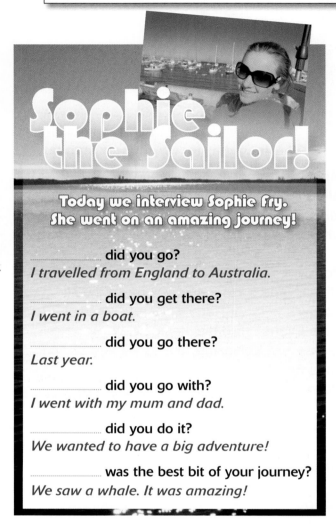

Sophie the Sailor!

Today we interview Sophie Fry. She went on an amazing journey!

.... did you go?
I travelled from England to Australia.

.... did you get there?
I went in a boat.

.... did you go there?
Last year.

.... did you go with?
I went with my mum and dad.

.... did you do it?
We wanted to have a big adventure!

.... was the best bit of your journey?
We saw a whale. It was amazing!

5 ☆ Work in pairs. Act out the conversation. Try to add more information.

6 ☆ Ask and answer questions about last week.

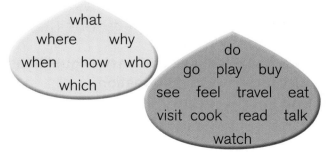

what
where   why
when   how   who
which

do
go   play   buy
see   feel   travel   eat
visit   cook   read   talk
watch

A What did you do on Saturday?
B I went ice skating.

7 Complete the conversation with the correct form of the past simple.

Jasmine interviewed her grandparents for a school project …

Jasmine When ¹........... you and Gran teenagers? (be)

Grandad A long time ago! It ²........... the late 1950s. (be)

Jasmine What ³........... you ....? (wear)

Grandad I ⁴........... jeans. (wear) And I ⁵........... a cool black jacket. (have)

Jasmine ⁶........... you .... to music? (listen)

Grandad Yes, I did. I ⁷........... rock 'n' roll. (like) And your gran ⁸........... Elvis Presley! (love)

Jasmine ⁹........... you .... to music at home? (listen)

Gran Yes, I did. We ¹⁰........... records on a record player at home. (play)

Jasmine What ¹¹........... you .... in the evenings? (do)

Gran I ¹²........... TV with the family. (watch) I ¹³........... (not play) computer games because there ¹⁴........... (not be) any computers! And we ¹⁵........... mobile phones. (not have) At the weekends we ¹⁶........... to dances and the cinema. (go)

Jasmine Thank you, that's great!

8 ◎ **1.40** **Listen and check.**

⟩ **Language check page 129**

Nouns and adjectives

9 Read the captions and complete the table.

Noun	Adjective
danger	dangerous
happiness	
strength	
noise	
safety	
health	

Phew. I'm safe!

You're very healthy!

You're happy today.

It's my birthday!

He's very strong!

It's very noisy in this car!

Putt Putt

Don't touch it. It's dangerous.

10 ⟨Circle⟩ the correct word.

1 I think the most important thing in life is **happy** / ⟨**happiness**⟩.

2 Dan won the judo competition. He's really **strength** / **strong**.

3 This road is very **danger** / **dangerous**.

4 Exercise is good for your **health** / **healthy**.

5 What is that horrible **noise** / **noisy**?

6 We learn about road **safety** / **safe** at school.

Reading and vocabulary

1 **Warm up** Look at the pictures. Find the things below.

• a knight • an archer • a chariot • a sword • a dragon • a magician

⊙ 1.42

Three British Heroes

King Arthur

was only 15 when he did an incredible thing. He pulled a sword out of a stone … and became king! Later, Merlin the magician took Arthur to a mysterious lake. Then a woman gave him another sword with special powers – Excalibur! He had a beautiful palace at Camelot and his knights sat with him at a round table. They had many adventures. They saved princesses, fought with bad knights, and killed dragons. At the end of his life, Arthur returned to the lake and a boat took him to the island of Avalon.

Robin Hood

was a thief and he didn't like rules – but English people loved him! His great enemy was the nasty Sheriff of Nottingham. Robin didn't live in a house. He lived in the middle of Sherwood Forest with his gang. His best friends were Little John and Will Scarlet. Maid Marian was his true love. He wore green clothes and was a fantastic archer. He could hit a small object from 300 metres! Robin and his men robbed rich people and gave their money to poor people.

Boudicca

was the queen of the Iceni tribe in Britain. She was very tall and had long red hair. She wore a lot of gold and rode a chariot. In AD 60 the Ancient Romans ruled Britain and asked the people for money (taxes). But Boudicca hated the Romans and she decided to fight. She had an army of 30,000 men and they attacked the city of London. The Romans had a smaller army, but they beat the British army and killed thousands of Britons. The Romans tried to catch Boudicca but she drank poison and died.

2 ○ **1.42** **Read and listen to the article on page 36 and complete the sentences with B (Boudicca), A (Arthur) or R (Robin).**

1 _R_ gave money to poor people.
2 _____ was the queen of a British tribe.
3 _____ lived in a beautiful palace.
4 _____ wore clothes of a special colour.
5 _____ became king when he was a teenager.
6 _____ lived in a forest.
7 _____ fought the Ancient Romans.
8 _____ died on an island in a lake.

Study skills

Before you read
Use pictures and headings to help you guess what the text is about. Who do you think is in the pictures on page 36? Look at the title. Where are these heroes from?

Listening and speaking

3 ○ **1.43** **Listen to the radio programme. Some people are talking about their heroes. Circle the correct words in the notes.**

Mary Shelley	
where from	England / USA
occupation	doctor / writer
why you admire him/her	She was only 18 / 21 when she started *Frankenstein*. She had an exciting / interesting life.

Pelé	
Spain / Brazil	
tennis player / footballer	
He was a creative / strong player. He played in the World Cup when he was 16 / 17.	

Tim Berners-Lee	
London / Manchester	
artist / scientist	
He invented / discovered the World Wide Web. He's really clever / shy.	

4 **Who is your hero? Think of a person you admire, alive or dead. Make notes.**

• name   Venus Williams
• where from   the USA
• occupation   she is a tennis player
• why you admire him or her   she is very strong and talented

5 **Work with a partner. Talk about your hero.**

Writing

6 **Write a paragraph about your hero. Include the information from Exercise 4.**

4A We're faster than you!

Grammar
comparative adjectives • *as … as /
not as … as*
Functions
making comparisons

Vocabulary • Nature

1 ⊙ **2.02** **Match the words with the pictures. Then listen and check.**

grass ☐   tree ☐   plant ☐   bird box ☑ 1   fence ☐
pond ☐   gate ☐   path ☐   flower bed ☐   bench ☐

2 **Look at the photos on page 39. Which of the things can you find?**

Presentation

3 **Warm up Read the information about Africa Challenge on page 39 and answer the questions.**

1 What does the team want to make?   **2** How much do people pay?

4 ⊙ **2.03** **Listen and read the photo story. Then answer the questions. Write *P* (Poppy), *A* (Alice), *J* (Jack) or *H* (Harry).**

Who …

1 … is collecting rubbish?   J, P, A and H   **4** … is digging a pond?
2 … has got a bigger bag?   **5** … thinks boys are stronger than girls?
3 … is holding a cricket bat?   **6** … is relaxing?

5 **Read *Language focus* and <u>underline</u> other examples of comparatives in the photo story.**

6 **Complete the sentences with your ideas. Then compare with your partner.**

Robert Pattinson   Shaun White   Barack Obama
David Beckham   Thandie Newton   Willow Smith
Maria Sharapova   Anne Hathaway

1 .... is taller than ....
2 .... is older than ....
3 .... is more famous than ....
4 .... is younger than ....
5 .... is more beautiful than ....

Language focus

• We're **faster** than you.
• Our bag is **bigger** than yours.
• Your job is **less difficult** than ours.
• It's **more important**.
• We're **as fast as** you.
• But you're **not as clever as** us!

Africa Challenge
Help us make a nature garden at our school ... and give money to the Africa Challenge! Just pay £2.

A 🔘 2.03 **First, the team collect rubbish.**

Jack We're faster than you!
Alice No, you're not! We're as fast as you.
Harry Look! Our bag's full of rubbish.
Alice Yeah, but our bag's bigger than yours!
Poppy And it's heavier, too! Look at this. It's a cricket bat!

B **Then Jack and Harry dig a pond. Alice and Poppy build bird boxes.**

Alice Your job's less difficult than ours.
Harry No way! It's more difficult. And it's dirtier!
Jack Anyway, only boys can dig a good pond.
Poppy Why?
Jack Because boys are stronger than girls!
Poppy That isn't true! And boys aren't as clever as girls.
Jack Ha ha. Very funny.
Alice Come on, you two. Let's put up the bird boxes!

C **Jack is busy ... but what about the girls?**

Jack Fantastic! Our bird box is higher than yours.
Poppy No, it isn't.
Harry Hey, what are you doing?
Alice Chill out! We finished ten minutes ago. We're relaxing.
Poppy It's better than working!

Your Space Making comparisons

7 Compare people in your family. Use these words.

taller stronger more intelligent younger older shorter funnier

My cousin Paul is younger than me.
My father is more intelligent than my grandfather.

Chat zone
No way!
Anyway,
Chill out!

Comparative adjectives

1 **Look at the pictures and write Max, Lara, Zak or Robopet. Use the table to help you.**

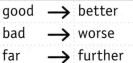

cold	→	cold**er**
strong	→	strong**er**
late	→	late**r**
nice	→	nice**r**
hot	→	hot**ter**
big	→	big**ger**
dirty	→	dirt**ier**
happy	→	happ**ier**
intelligent	→	**more** intelligent
beautiful	→	**more** beautiful

good	→	better
bad	→	worse
far	→	further

.... is more artistic than ....
.... is taller than ....

Woof!!!!
Woof!!!!

.... is more intelligent than ....
.... is noisier than ....

2 ✎ **Write sentences comparing the things below. Then compare your sentences with a partner's. Use these adjectives.**

exciting	cheap	small	good
difficult	fast	cheerful	silly
beautiful	dangerous	strong	
interesting	hot	tall	cold
boring	old	big	expensive

Films are better than books.
Maths is more difficult than English.

books / films

English / Maths

cars / bikes

football / rugby

summer / winter

you / your best friend

Batman / Superman

London / New York

Soundbite

/ɒ/ /əʊ/

a ◉ **2.04 Listen and repeat.**
1 D**o**n't dr**o**p litter, take it h**o**me!
2 There's a photo of a bottle on my mobile phone.
3 Yoghurt pots can get stuck on their bodies.
4 I want to go swimming at my local beach.

b ◉ **2.04 Listen again. Circle the /ɒ/ sounds and underline the /əʊ/ sounds.**

3 ⭐ **Work in pairs. Do the quiz.**

A I think the River Amazon is longer than the River Nile.

B I agree. / I don't agree.

What do you know?

long
the River Nile — the River Amazon

tall
the Eiffel Tower — the Statue of Liberty

intelligent
parrots — hamsters

old
Stonehenge — the Colosseum

fast
snails — tortoises

big
Australia — Japan

4 🔘 **2.05** **Listen and check your answers. Then write true sentences.**

The River Amazon is longer than the River Nile.

as ... as / not as .... as

Jake	is is**n't**	**as**	strong	**as**	Henry
Cats	are are**n't**	**as**	friendly	**as**	dogs
Is Elena		**as**	tall	**as**	Chiara?
Are bikes		**as**	fast	**as**	cars?

5 **Rewrite the sentences with *(not) as*.**

1 Elephants are heavier than lions.
Lions aren't as heavy as elephants.

2 Leo is 14. Max is 14 too.

3 Horror films are more exciting than romantic films.

4 Rio de Janeiro is bigger than Warsaw.

5 Monkeys are more intelligent than cats.

6 Beyoncé is 30. Shakira is 34.

7 The Atacama desert is drier than the Sahara.

6 ✏️ **Look at the table and write sentences comparing Max with Bob.**

	Max	Bob
1	5 years old	3 years old
2	30cm tall	1m tall
3	very intelligent	not very intelligent
4	not very fit	very fit
5	isn't fast	is fast
6	very noisy	not very noisy

1 *Max is older than Bob.*
Bob is not as old as Max.

7 ⭐ **Compare yourself with a friend or a member of your family. Write six sentences. Tell your partner.**

I'm younger than my sister.
I'm as tall as my mum.

Vocabulary • Geography

1 ⊙ **2.06** Match the words with the places on the map. Then listen and check.

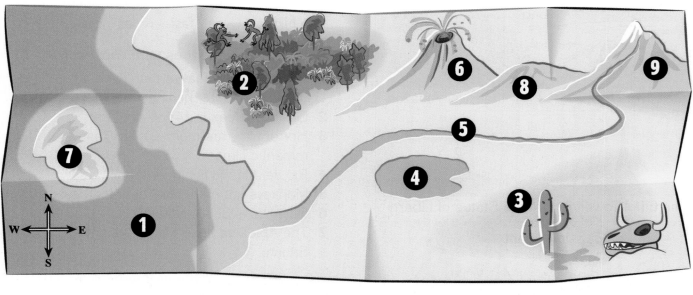

sea 1   river ☐   desert ☐   island ☐   mountain ☐
lake ☐   volcano ☐   rainforest ☐   hill ☐

2 Work with a partner. Can you think of examples of these places?

A river – The River Thames

Presentation

3 ⊙ **2.07** Do the quiz on page 43. Listen and check your answers. How many did you get right?

4 Read *Language focus*. <u>Underline</u> other examples of superlative adjectives in the quiz.

5 Work in groups. Answer the questions about your country, then tell the class what you think. You can check your answers on the internet.

What is the longest river?

What is the most crowded city?

What is the hottest place?

What is the coldest place?

What is the highest mountain?

Language focus

- Where is **the coldest** place in the world?
- **The longest** river in the world is 6,695 kilometres long.
- Which is **the most crowded** city in the world?
- What is **the most dangerous** volcano in the world?

The greatest quiz about Planet Earth ...ever!

The world is an amazing place – but how well do you know it? Do our quiz and find out!

1 Where is the coldest place in the world?
a Russia
b Antarctica
c The Arctic

2 Which is the biggest hot desert in the world?
a The Gobi Desert
b The Kalahari Desert
c The Sahara Desert

3 In some places it rains very little. Where is the driest place in the world?
a Chile
b Egypt
c China

4 The highest mountain in the world is Mount Everest. But where is it?
a the Andes
b the Himalayas
c the Alps

5 Many cities have millions of people. Which is the most crowded city in the world?
a Mexico City
b Shanghai
c Tokyo

6 Which country has the most lakes in the world?
a Canada
b China
c the USA

7 Where can you find the most dangerous spider in the world?
a South America
b Europe
c Africa

8 The deepest point under the sea is in the Pacific Ocean. But how deep is it?
a 4,200 metres
b 7,508 metres
c 10,911 metres

9 The longest river in the world is 6,695 kilometres long. But which river is it?
a The Amazon, South America
b The Chang Jiang (Yangtze), China
c The Nile, Africa

10 In some countries it rains a lot! Where is the wettest place in the world?
a Ireland
b India
c Brazil

SCORE

8—10
Congratulations!
You are a Planet Earth Expert!

4—7
Well done! *Do you want to travel round the world?*

0—3
Oh dear! *It's time to study Geography!*

Your Space   Making comparisons

6 Work in pairs. Discuss these questions.

In your opinion, who or what is ... ?

- the most exciting film
- the biggest room in your school
- the funniest actor
- the most interesting TV programme
- the most beautiful building in your town
- the best singer

The most beautiful building in our town is the library.

7 Work in groups. Compare your ideas.

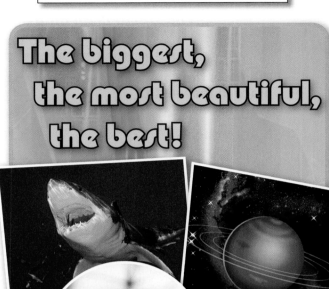

4B 🔳 Language space

Superlative adjectives

long	→	the long**est**
safe	→	the saf**est**
wet	→	the wet**test**
hungry	→	the hungr**iest**
important	→	the **most** important

good	→	the best
bad	→	the worst
far	→	the furthest

1 **Look at the cartoons and number the sentences. Use the tables to help you.**

I'm the smallest. ☐
I'm the most famous. ☐
I'm the happiest. ☐
I'm the fastest. ☐

2 **Write the superlative form of the adjectives.**

> high   happy   good
> famous   popular   wide
> big   boring   bad
> tall   busy   beautiful

high → the highest

3 **Complete the sentences with the superlative form of these adjectives.**

> big   far   intelligent   deep
> old   noisy   poisonous   famous

The biggest, the most beautiful, the best!

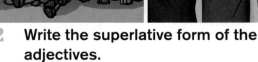

1 The _biggest_ fish in the world is the white shark.
2 Dolphins are one of the _____ animals.
3 At 1,637 metres, Lake Baikal in Siberia is the _____ in the world.
4 The planet _____ from the Sun is Neptune.
5 The world's _____ land snake is the king cobra.
6 The world's _____ tree started growing 4,000 years ago!
7 The _____ animals are the howler monkeys of South America. You can hear them five kilometres away!
8 The _____ monster in a lake is Nessie, the Loch Ness Monster!

4 Write the superlative form of the adjectives. Then complete with your ideas.

Quick Questionnaire

In my opinion...

1 The most difficult (difficult) sport is water polo.

2 _____ (funny) TV programme is

3 _____ (dangerous) sport is

4 _____ (scary) animal is

5 _____ (beautiful) building is

6 _____ (bad) day of the week is

7 _____ (exciting) film is

8 _____ (delicious) food is

9 _____ (good) month of the year is

10 _____ (interesting) school subject is

5 Work in pairs. Ask and answer questions.

A In your opinion, what's the most interesting school subject?
B Maths!

Get it right!

Use the correct form for superlative adjectives:
He's the best football player in the world.
NOT ~~He's the better football player in the world~~.
Olivia is the tallest girl in the class.
NOT ~~Olivia is the taller girl in the class.~~

Prefixes: *un*

We can add the prefix *un* to the beginning of an adjective to give the opposite meaning.

unhappy   **un**popular

unwell   **un**fit

friendly	**un**friendly
safe	**un**safe
kind	**un**kind
fair	**un**fair

6 Complete the sentences with an adjective.

1 Harvey hasn't got any friends.
He's _unpopular_ .
2 My brother never does any exercise.
He's _____ .
3 Don't ride that bike! It's _____ .
4 Lucy isn't at school today. She's _____ .
5 Billy often says horrible things.
He's _____ .
6 We had too much homework at the weekend.
It's _____ .
7 Chloe can't go swimming because it's raining.
She's _____ .
8 My next-door neighbour never says hello.
She's _____ .

Vocabulary and listening • Animals

1 ⊙ **2.09** **Match the words with the pictures. Then listen and check.**

wing ☐   tail ☐   feathers ☐   fur ☐   claw ☐
paw ☐   nose ☐   hoof (hooves) ☐ 1   beak ☐   tooth (teeth) ☐

2 ⊙ **2.10** **Listen to the descriptions of the animals and number them in the order you hear them.**

horse ☐   bear ☐   ostrich ☐   tiger ☐   bat ☐   snake ☐

Reading

3 **Warm up** **Look at the article on page 47. Read the headings 1–4 and match them with the pictures.**

4 **Read the article again and decide if the sentences are true (*T*) or false (*F*).**

1 Litter can hurt animals.   *T*
2 Four-pack rings are really useful for animals.
3 Birds like eating chewing gum.
4 Plastic bags are very bad for marine animals and sea birds.
5 It's difficult for animals to go into bottles and cans.

5 **Complete the summary of the article with these words.**

> animals   carefully   throw   eat   hurt   stuck   ~~dangerous~~

Litter is very ¹ _dangerous_ for birds and animals. Four-pack rings can get
² _____ on their bodies. Chewing gum and plastic bags can ³ _____
birds. Marine animals can ⁴ _____ plastic bags and get sick. And bottles
and cans can kill small ⁵ _____ . We can ⁶ _____ our litter away
⁷ _____ and clean up our local area.

ANIMALS AT RISK

Litter is ugly. But did you know it can hurt wildlife? Make sure you throw away all your rubbish carefully. You can also organise litter collection days at your school or in your area.

1. Four-pack rings – no fun for birds

Plastic drink rings are really useful to people, but birds can put their heads through the rings and then get stuck. They can't find food or eat. But you can help. First cut each ring with scissors, and then put them in the bin.

2. Chewing gum – a sticky problem

Chewing gum makes a terrible mess. And it can hurt birds. So be careful where you put it. The gum gets stuck to a bird's beak or feathers, and then it can't eat or keep clean.

3. Plastic bags – plastic snacks

There are millions of plastic bags in the sea and they can hurt marine animals and sea birds. Scientists find lots of plastic inside their stomachs, and sometimes the bags get stuck on their legs and wings. So be careful where you throw your plastic bags.

4. Bottles and cans – not a great home

There are lots of bottles and cans in the countryside. And small animals think, 'What a great place to live!' It is easy for them to go in but difficult for them to get out! So take those empty bottles and cans home and recycle them.

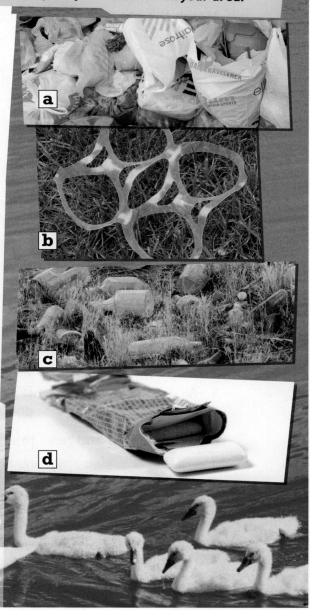

Speaking and writing

6 Work in groups. Discuss the questions.

- Which type of litter is the biggest problem in your school / the local park / your town / the local countryside?
- What can you do about litter in your school / in your town / on your local beach?

7 Write a paragraph about litter problems where you live.

The biggest litter problem where I live is …
There is also litter …

Communication page 111

Your Space Web Zone

Study skills

Before you speak
Plan what you want to say before you speak. Choose the best grammar and vocabulary. Get help if you don't know words.

5A We're going for a pizza

Grammar
present continuous for future arrangements • *would like (to)*

Functions
talking about future plans

Vocabulary • Things to do

1 Match the places with the pictures.

a boat trip ☐   a museum ☐   a theme park ☐   a restaurant ☐   shops ☐   a park ☐

Presentation

2 **Warm up** Look at the photos on page 49 and answer the questions.

1 Who is in pictures A and B? What are they doing?

2 What are Jack and Alice doing in picture C?

3 🔊 **2.13** Listen and read the photo story on page 49. Then answer the questions.

1 What time is Harry meeting his brother?   *At half past five.*

2 What film is on at the cinema?

3 Who is Poppy going shopping with?

4 Who is 21 years old tomorrow?

5 Who likes going on boats?

6 Who hasn't got any fixed plans?

4 Read *Language focus*. Then complete the conversation with the correct form of the verb.

Harry Hi Jack. What ¹ _are you doing_ (do) tomorrow?

Jack I ² _____ (play) football in the morning. And in the afternoon I ³ _____ (see) my mate Charlie. We ⁴ _____ (write) songs together. ⁵ _____ (you / go) to the park tomorrow morning?

Harry No, I ⁶ _____ . In fact, I ⁷ _____ (not do) any sport this weekend.

Jack Why not?

Harry We ⁸ _____ (visit) my aunt and uncle in Brighton. And I don't want to go!

Jack Oh, poor you.

> **Language focus**
> - **I'm meeting** my brother at half past five.
> - **We're staying** in London on Saturday night.
> - **What are you doing** this afternoon?
> - **Is Jack going** to the cinema with you?
> - No, **he isn't.**

A **2.13 It's Friday afternoon. Poppy chats with Harry after school.**

Poppy What are you doing this afternoon, Harry?

Harry I'm going to the cinema. I'm meeting my brother at half past five.

Poppy What film are you seeing?

Harry The new Batman film. Then we're going for a pizza. Would you like to come?

Poppy I'd love to, but I can't. I'm going shopping with my mum.

Harry What are you getting?

Poppy We're buying presents for my cousin Kate. It's her twenty-first birthday tomorrow.

Harry Really? Is she having a birthday party?

Poppy Yes, she is! She's having a huge party in London!

Harry Cool!

B **Poppy talks about her plans.**

Harry When are you leaving?

Poppy Tomorrow morning. We're staying in London on Saturday night and coming back on Sunday. But we're visiting museums and stuff first. And we're going on a boat trip on the River Thames. My brother's mad about boats! Anyway, is Jack going to the cinema with you?

Harry No, he isn't. He's got other plans. You know, the Challenge!

Poppy What are you doing this afternoon, Alice?

Alice I don't know. Have a good weekend!

C **Later, Poppy is shopping in the town centre. And she has a surprise.**

Hey, that's Alice and she's with Jack.

Your Space Talking about next weekend

5 **What are your plans for the weekend? Choose from the places in Exercise 1, then tell your partner. Are you doing the same things?**

A What are you doing at the weekend?
B I'm going shopping.
A Me too. What time are you going?

A I'm going to a theme park.
B I'm not. I'm playing football in the park with Tom.

Chat zone

Really?
mad about ...
anyway

Future arrangements

1 **Complete the conversation with the verbs below. Use the table to help you.**

> I'm making   are you doing
> I'm going   like to

What are you doing tomorrow evening?
I'm meeting my aunt.
Would you like to come to the cinema?
Yes, I would. / Yes, I'd love to.
Would you like to come to my party on Saturday?
No, I'm sorry I can't. I'm busy.

What .... this evening?

.... a cake for Lara. What about you?

.... to a fancy dress party. Would you .... come with me?

2 ⊙ **2.14** **Sam Tyler talks to his agent about his plans. Listen and match the times with his plans.**

this afternoon

tonight   this evening

next week   in March

tomorrow   next year

the day after tomorrow

go to New Zealand to meet fans
go to the gym with his trainer
fly to New York for a concert
sing in a concert in New York
go to a party at Madonna's house
have coffee with Simon Cowell
write the story of his life
have dinner with Jessica Alba

3 ✎ **Write sentences about Sam's plans.**

This afternoon Sam is having coffee with Simon Cowell.

Sam Tyler

4 🗨 **Work in pairs. Choose A or B. Then cover the other diary. Arrange to do two things together.**

A Would you like to go swimming on Monday morning?

B I'm sorry, I can't. I'm playing tennis. Would you like to go to the cinema on Friday afternoon?

A Yes, I would. That's a great idea!

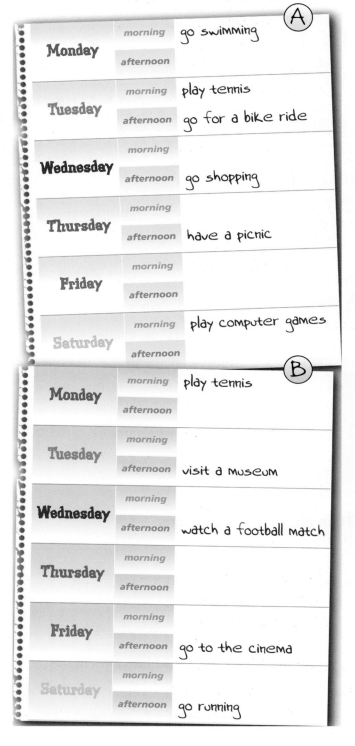

Get it right!

Would you like to see my photos?
Yes, I would.   NOT   ~~Yes, I would like.~~
Would you like a sweet?
Yes, please.   NOT   ~~Yes, I like.~~

5 (Circle) **the correct answer.**

1 Would you like to play tennis with me?
  a No, I wouldn't.
  b No, I'm sorry, I've got my guitar lesson.

2 Would you like some orange juice?
  a Yes, I like.   **b** Yes, please.

3 Would you like to come to my house this afternoon?
  a No, I'm sorry. I'm doing my homework.
  b No, I wouldn't.

6 🗨 **Work in pairs. Make invitations or offers and short answers. Use the pictures to help you.**

A Would you like some fruit?
B Yes, I would.
A Would you like to … ?

Grammar
may / might • present continuous • infinitive of purpose

Functions
talking about future plans

Vocabulary • Shops

1 ⊙ **2.15** **Match the words with the pictures. Then listen and check.**

pharmacy ☐   bookshop ☐   supermarket ☐   shoe shop ☐
music store ☐   greengrocer's ☐   sports shop ☐   clothes shop ☐
mobile phone shop ☐   newsagent's ☐   butcher's ☐   games shop ☐

2 **Work with a partner. Look at the shopping list. Ask your partner where you can buy these things. You can invent more questions.**

A Where do you go to buy trainers?
B A shoe shop or a sports shop. Where do you go to buy a dictionary?
A A bookshop. Where ... ?

Shopping List
mobile phone
trainers
a computer game
a dictionary
a T-shirt
medicine and make-up
oranges
a tennis racquet
a DVD
beef
magazines
cakes
food and drink

Presentation

3 **Warm up** **Look quickly at page 53.**

What do you think the article is about? Where do you think the people live?

4 ⊙ **2.16** **Read and listen to the article. Then answer the questions.**

1 How does Theo feel?   *A bit tired.*
2 What does Naomi need? Why?
3 What is Harvey doing on Saturday afternoon?
4 Why isn't Alisha buying anything?
5 What does Brandon do on Saturdays?
6 Where is Caitlin working?

5 **Read *Language focus*. Who is sure (✓) and who isn't sure (?) about their plans for Saturday? Write the names.**   *? Theo   ✓ Naomi*

Language focus

• I **might** go to the sports centre.
• We **might** hang out in the shopping centre.
• I **may** see a film.

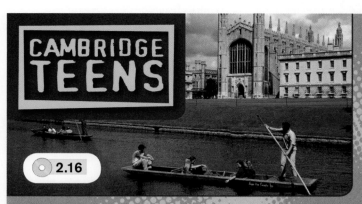

2.16

What are you doing on Saturday?

Theo

Saturday? I don't know. I might go to the sports centre. But I feel a bit tired so I might stay in bed in the morning!

Naomi

I'm meeting my friends in town and then we're going shopping! I need new jeans. Look at these! They're old and horrible! And there's a cool new clothes shop I want to go to.

Harvey

It's my birthday on Saturday! So I'm going for a pizza with my family at lunchtime and then in the afternoon I'm going to a football match with my friends.

Alisha

I might play computer games at home with my friend Amy. Or we might hang out in the shopping centre. I don't have any money at the moment so I'm not buying anything!

Brandon

I'm meeting friends in the big book shop in town. You know, the one with the café? We often have a drink there and look at the music and sport magazines.

Caitlin

I'm working! I've got a Saturday job in a sports shop. But in the evening I may see a film with my boyfriend. I'm not sure.

Have you got any plans for an exciting Saturday?
Send an email or a text to let us know!

Your Space Talking about your plans

6 **Work in pairs. Talk about your plans and ideas for this evening. Use:**

- the present continuous for definite plans
- *may / might* when you are not sure

A What are you doing this evening?
B I'm having a piano lesson at six o'clock. What about you?
A I don't know. I might see my friend, Jonah, or I may read a book.

Talking about future plans

- Use the present continuous when you are sure.
- Use *may / might* when you are not sure.

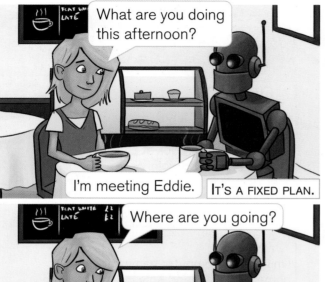

What are you doing this afternoon?

I'm meeting Eddie. IT'S A FIXED PLAN.

Where are you going?

I don't know. We might go to the park or we might watch a film. IT'S NOT SURE.

1 Complete the sentences.

may not play   may watch   might not go
may have   might eat   might not finish
~~might do~~   might not call

1 I _might do_ my homework on the computer.
2 We _____ an ice cream after football practice.
3 Jessica is very busy so she _____ to London tomorrow.
4 I _____ this new DVD after dinner this evening.
5 Brad _____ me on his mobile because it's expensive in the morning.
6 I don't like this book. I _____ it.
7 I'm not well. I _____ football with my friends today in the park.
8 Jack _____ another pizza. He's very hungry.

2 ⊙ 2.17 Brandon is talking about his plans for the week. Listen and complete the planner with a tick (✓) for sure or a question mark (?) for not sure.

Weekly Planner

Monday	play volleyball ☐
Tuesday	go to Tom's house ☐
Wednesday	watch a DVD ☐
Thursday	do History homework ☐
Friday	go to computer club ☐
Saturday	play football ☐
Sunday	visit Grandma ☐

3 ✎ Write sentences about Brandon's plans.

Brandon might play football on Saturday.

4 ✍ Work in pairs. Copy and complete a weekly planner for you. Then ask and answer questions with your partner.

A What are you doing on Monday?
B I might go to the swimming pool after school.

Soundbite

Word stress

a ⊙ 2.18 Listen and repeat.
bookshop   sports shop
shoe shop   music store
tennis racquet   memory card
swimming pool   computer game
changing room   newsagent's

b ⊙ 2.18 Listen again and underline the stressed syllables.

Infinitive of purpose

5 Look at the pictures. What do you use these things for? Use the phrases below.

> to take photos   to play tennis
> to pay for things   to paint pictures
> to tell the time   to do sums
> to write on a computer
> ~~to make phone calls~~

1 You use a mobile phone to make phone calls.

1

2

3

4

5

6

7

8

6 ☆ Work in pairs. What do you use these for?

> scissors | glasses | pencil case
> bed | toothbrush | cup | keys

Language check page 130

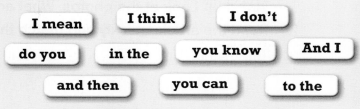

Word chunks

Some groups of words (chunks) are very common in English. And they're very easy words!

> I mean   I think   I don't
> do you   in the   you know   And I
> and then   you can   to the

7 Underline the word chunks in the conversation.

Tyler Hi, what are you doing tomorrow?

Isabel Well, I don't know. I think we're going shopping.

Tyler Right. Do you like shopping on Saturday?

Isabel Yeah, I mean, it's OK. And I sometimes buy a game or a DVD. And then we often go to the cinema.

Tyler Oh, which one?

Isabel You know, the big multiplex in the shopping centre. You can have a hamburger there, too.

8 Complete the sentences with one of these phrases.

> I think   do you   to the   I mean
> ~~you can~~   and then

1 _You can_ buy really cheap music on this website.
2 On Friday I usually go _____ school orchestra practice.
3 **A** _____ like scary horror films?
   B Yes, I do.
4 I've got a new computer. _____, it's not really new. It was my dad's.
5 Yesterday morning we went for a walk. _____ we had a roast dinner in the evening.
6 **A** What's the capital of Spain?
   B _____ it's Madrid.

5C Skills

Reading and speaking

1 **Warm up** Look at the photos. What activities can you see? Which ones do you like?

2 Read the article quickly and match the headings with the activities.

Top of the world ☐   The secrets of sport ☐

Winter indoors ☐   *Be a time traveller* ☐

Fantastic Days Out

Home   For kids   **For teens**   For schools   Contact   Links

A Do you want to travel in time? Do you want to meet Vikings? You can, at the **Jorvik Viking Centre** in York in the north of England. Go back in time to 25 October, AD 975! Experience the smells

and the sounds of over 1,000 years ago. See Viking homes, shops, streets and people in their daily life – working, cooking, and playing!

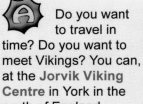

B Take an amazing tour of the **Manchester United 'Theatre of Dreams' stadium and museum.** Learn about the history of this world-famous club, see all the trophies, have fun with the interactive show, and become a

TV sports commentator for the club's most exciting goals. Learn more about professional footballers when you visit the changing rooms, learn about their favourite food, go to the VIP lounge, and walk through the Red Tunnel onto the football pitch.

C Is the weather hot? Are you bored with the swimming pool, but love water? You should go to **Quaywest Water Park** in Devon. There are lots of exciting slides and rides there

– and you always get very wet! Try the Wet and Wild slide first, it's fast but great fun. And why not try the Devil's Drop waterslide? The slide is 20 metres high and very fast! You can also go on the Surf Lagoon sitting on a tyre.

D It doesn't snow much in Milton Keynes, but you can ski on real snow every day of the year at **SNO!zone**. The slope is 170 metres long! It's cold, too, so you must wear warm clothes. You can learn to ski or snowboard or just

practise your winter sports skills. There's skiing fun for all the family!

3 **Read the article again and answer the questions.**

Where can you …
1 … go down a 170-metre slope?
   At SNO!zone
2 … go back in time 1,000 years?
3 … get very wet?
4 … learn to ski?

5 … visit a football stadium?
6 … see how people lived in the past?
7 … go down a 20-metre slide?
8 … see football trophies?

4 **Choose the best day out for these people.**

1 Mia and Fatima enjoy ice skating. They like skiing too.
2 Ethan loves swimming and doing exciting things.
3 Lucas loves history and stories about the past.
4 Enrico loves sport. He is a great football fan.

5 **Choose your favourite day out. Compare with your partner.**
Do you want to do the same things?

Listening

6 **2.20** **Listen and complete the information about Jorvik.**

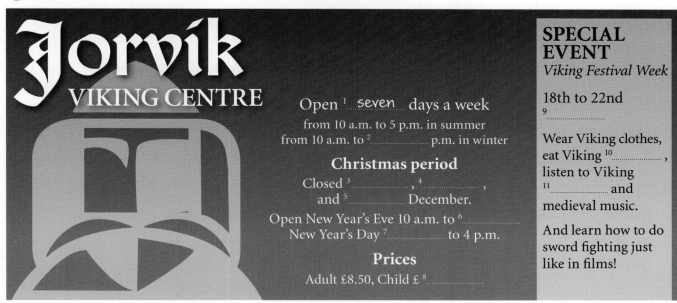

Jorvík VIKING CENTRE

Open ¹ _seven_ days a week
from 10 a.m. to 5 p.m. in summer
from 10 a.m. to ² _____ p.m. in winter

Christmas period
Closed ³ _____ , ⁴ _____ ,
and ⁵ _____ December.
Open New Year's Eve 10 a.m. to ⁶ _____
New Year's Day ⁷ _____ to 4 p.m.

Prices
Adult £8.50, Child £ ⁸ _____

SPECIAL EVENT
Viking Festival Week
18th to 22nd
⁹ _____

Wear Viking clothes, eat Viking ¹⁰ _____ , listen to Viking ¹¹ _____ and medieval music.

And learn how to do sword fighting just like in films!

Writing

7 **Write an email to a friend. It's Saturday evening. Tell him/her what you did today and what you are planning to do on Sunday.**

Include:
• what you did today
• what you liked / didn't like
   Start:
   Hi (name)
   How are you?

• what you are doing on Sunday
• who you are doing it with
   Finish:
   take care / see you soon
   (your name)

Communication page 112

 Your Space Web Zone

Study skills

Writing an email
Remember to write a subject.
Open your email to a friend with: *Hi!* or *Dear* + name.
Close your email with: *Take care* or *See you soon.*

6A You mustn't watch TV

Vocabulary • TV programmes

1   ⊙ **2.23** **Read the TV guide and match the programmes with the words below. Then listen and check.**

1 sports programme   **2** quiz show   **3** cartoon   **4** nature programme   **5** documentary
6 the news   **7** reality show   **8** comedy   **9** soap opera   **10** talent show

3.30 p.m.	**Amazing Animals** Ellie swims with dolphins in Australia. ☐	
4.30 p.m.	**The Simpsons** Bart goes camping! ☐	
5 p.m.	**20 Questions** This week's celebrity teams find the answers! ☐	
6 p.m.	**News and weather** ☐	
6.30 p.m.	**Home Sweet Home** Cheryl is angry with Max. And Pete has a surprise. ☐	
7 p.m.	**Big Brother** More real-life action. Who is leaving the house tonight? ☐	

8 p.m.	**Make Me a Star** The last two contestants sing for the prize. ☐
10 p.m.	**Iggy and Ted** More madness from the comedy duo. ☐
10.35 p.m.	**The Big Match** Manchester United v Juventus. ☐ 1
11.30 p.m.	**American Presidents** Part 6 The Kennedy years. ☐

2   **Work with a partner. Discuss which programmes you like and dislike.**

A I really like cartoons.   **B** I don't like soap operas. I think they're silly!

Presentation

3   **Warm up Look at the photos on page 59.**

Who can you see? Where are they? What is Poppy doing in picture B?

4   ⊙ **2.24** **Listen and read the photo story on page 59. Then answer the questions.**

1 What are the rules for Alice's new Challenge?
2 How long is the Challenge?
3 Why does Poppy want to watch *Celebrity Chat*?
4 What is Poppy's new idea for a Challenge?

5   **Read *Language focus*. Then complete the rules for an exam in Poppy's school with *must* or *mustn't*. Use the verbs below.**

> **Language focus**
> • You **must** remember the rules.
> • We **mustn't** play computer games.
> • You **have to** do it.
> • You **don't have to** be bored.

look   answer   use   finish   talk   ~~be~~   write (x 2)

You ¹ *mustn't be* late. (✗)
You ² .... with a pen, not a pencil. (✓)
You ³ .... to other students. (✗)
You ⁴ .... your name at the top of the page. (✓)

You ⁵ .... a mobile phone. (✗)
You ⁶ .... all the questions. (✓)
You ⁷ .... at other students' answers. (✗)
You ⁸ .... after 30 minutes. (✓)

A **2.24 The team has got a new idea for raising money. And Harry doesn't like it!**

Alice   Right, the rules are simple. We mustn't use the internet or our mobile phones. And we mustn't watch TV for a week.

Harry   You can't be serious! A whole week?

Alice   That's right.

Harry   No comedy programmes? Or cartoons?

Alice   Of course not.

Poppy   The worst thing is no texting. I love my mobile!

Harry   And I love TV.

Alice   Cheer up, Harry! TV's boring!

Poppy   So what can we do? Do we have to read books?

Alice   No, you don't. And you don't have to stay in your room. You can see your friends, play board games, do sport, listen to music …!

Jack   We have to do it. It's for the Challenge.

B   **Five days later …**

Poppy   Great! It's *Celebrity Chat*! My favourite programme!

Mum   I'm sorry, Poppy. You mustn't watch TV for another two days.

Poppy   Oh, please, Mum. I must watch it!

Mum   You have to remember the rules, Poppy!

Poppy   That's so unfair! I'm bored!

Mum   You don't have to be bored. You can come with me to the supermarket!

Poppy   Oh, thanks!

C   It's the end of the week and Poppy sends a text message to Jack.

That was the worst week of my life! I've got a great new idea. Let's do a pop concert! :)

Chat zone
You can't be serious!
The worst thing …
Cheer up!
That's so unfair!

Your Space   Talking about things you have to do

6   **Work in pairs. Tell your partner about the things you have to do this week.**

I have to do my homework. I have to make my bed every day. I have to take the dog for a walk.

must / have to

- In the positive, *have to* and *must* have similar meanings.

I must buy a birthday card for my sister!

- We can use *must* to talk about a personal obligation.

You mustn't go into the water, Max!

- Use *mustn't* for negative rules.

I have to go to the supermarket.

- We can use *have to* to talk about an obligation from someone else.

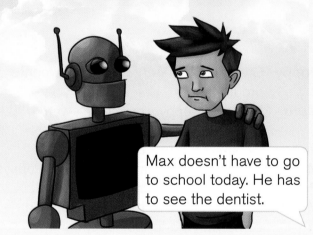

Max doesn't have to go to school today. He has to see the dentist.

- Use *don't have to* when there is no obligation.

1 Complete the school canteen rules with *must* or *mustn't* and one of these verbs.

eat	leave	~~wash~~	be
use	wait	put	

2 ✎ Write rules for your school.

My School Rules

School canteen rules

1 You <u>must wash</u> your hands before you eat.

2 You .... your turn to order food.

3 You .... rude to the staff in the canteen.

4 You .... your food quietly.

5 You .... your mobile phone in the canteen.

6 You .... plastic cups in the recycling bins.

7 You .... your tray on the table.

3 ◉ **2.25** Listen and tick (✓) the chores Harvey has to do, cross (✗) the chores he doesn't have to do.

tidy room ☐
take out the rubbish ☐
feed the hamster ☐
go to the library ☐
take the dog for a walk ☐
ring Gran ☐
do homework ☐

Get it right!

Mustn't and *don't have to* are different! *Mustn't* means you are prohibited from doing something. *Don't have to* means that it is not necessary to do something.
You don't have to bring anything.
NOT ~~You mustn't bring anything.~~
You don't have to wear special clothes.
NOT ~~You mustn't wear special clothes.~~

4 ✍ **Write sentences about Harvey.**

He has to feed the hamster.

5 💬 **Work in pairs. Roleplay a conversation between Harvey and his mother.**

A OK, Harvey. This is a list of the things you have to do.
B Do I have to tidy my room?

6 **Read and complete the questionnaire for you with ticks (✓).**

What do you have to do at home?

	have to	don't have to	mustn't
1 take out the rubbish	○	○	○
2 tidy my room	○	○	○
3 get up early on Sunday	○	○	○
4 play loud music in my room	○	○	○
5 make my bed	○	○	○
6 play video games all day	○	○	○
7 go to bed after 12 o'clock	○	○	○
8 do my homework every day	○	○	○
9 do exercise every day	○	○	○
10 help my parents in the kitchen	○	○	○

7 💬 **Work in pairs. Discuss your answers.**

A I have to make my bed.
B Really? I don't have to make my bed.

Soundbite

/hæv tə/

a ◉ **2.26** Listen and say the rap.

We have to talk,
I have to phone,
You have to text me,
I'm all alone!
He has to write,
She has to read,
They have to meet
As they agreed.

b **Write and say your own *have to* rap.**

6B What should you do?

Vocabulary • Computers

1 ⊙ **2.27 Match the words with the pictures. Then listen and check.**

mouse ☐ printer ☐ monitor ☐1 plug ☐ icon ☐ screen ☐
joystick ☐ keyboard ☐ cursor ☐ mouse mat ☐

2 **Work with a partner. Answer the questions.**

1 Have you got a computer at home? Where is it?
2 How often do you use a computer?
3 What picture is on your mouse mat at home?
4 What picture is on your screen?

Presentation

3 **Warm up Look at the quiz on page 63. What is it about?**

4 **Do the quiz on page 63, then check your answers. Do you think you are safe on the internet?**

5 **Read *Language focus*. Then read the students' problems. Complete the advice with *should* or *shouldn't*.**

1 I always arrive late for school.
You _should_ leave home earlier.
2 I can't wake up in the morning.
You _____ go to bed late.
3 I can't remember new words in English.
You _____ use a vocabulary notebook.
4 I often get bad marks for my homework.
You _____ watch TV all evening!
5 I've got an exam tomorrow and I'm really nervous.
You _____ worry. You _____ try to relax.

Language focus

• You **should** tell your parents.
• You **shouldn't** open it.
• What **should** you do?

BE SAFE BE HAPPY

The internet is fantastic. You can do lots of different things. But are you always safe on the web? What should you do?

Do our quiz and choose the best advice, a or b.

1 **You want to chat online. You need a screen name.**
a You should use an invented name.
b You should use your real name.

2 **You receive an email from a person you don't know. It's got an attachment.**
a You should open it and send it to your friends. It might be interesting!
b Don't open it. You should delete it immediately.

3 **A web pal says that they are your age.**
a You shouldn't always believe them.
b You should believe them.

4 **You are online.**
a You shouldn't tell people your address or phone number.
b It's OK to give your personal information.

5 **A website asks you to register with your personal details.**
a It's OK. Your information is safe on the internet.
b Check with your parents or carer first.

6 **A web pal wants to meet you.**
a You should tell your parents.
b You should meet them in secret.

7 **You have a blog.**
a You should put your personal photos on it.
b Be careful about the photos you share.

8 **You want to be safe on the internet.**
a You shouldn't use it! It's too dangerous.
b You should follow our advice and enjoy it!

SCORE

How safe are you? These are the safe answers.

1a 2b 3a 4a 5b 6a 7b 8b

Your Space   Talking about the internet

6 **What do you do on the internet? Tick (✓) the things you do.**

do research for your homework ☐   play games ☐   send emails ☐
chat with friends ☐   download music or games ☐   write a blog ☐
share your photos ☐   get news about celebrities ☐
watch TV programmes ☐

7 **Work in pairs. Compare your answers.**

should

1 Complete the cartoon with *should* or *shouldn't*.

What's wrong, Zak?

I'm scared!

You .... watch horror films!
You .... change the DVD!

2 Put the words in the correct order to make sentences.

1 copy / shouldn't / in tests / you
You shouldn't copy in tests.
2 wear / should / this dress / I ?
3 they / play loud music / shouldn't
4 should / drink two litres of water / you / a day

3 ⊙ **2.28** Listen to four teenagers talking about their problems on a radio phone-in programme. Match the problems 1–4 with the best advice.

☐ You shouldn't use her computer.

☐ You shouldn't download music.

☐ You shouldn't stay up late.

☐ You should listen more in class.

☐ You should take it for a walk.

☐ You should take it to the vet.

☐ You should keep a vocabulary notebook.

☐ You should use a dictionary.

4 ⊙ **2.29** Listen and check your answers.

5 📖 **Read the cartoons. Give advice using *should* / *shouldn't* and the phrases below.**

> see his new film   watch it   ~~do some sport~~
> wear a helmet   eat it   go to the hairdresser's
> buy so many clothes

1

I feel really unfit.

You should do some sport.

2

I often fall off my bike.

3

This cheese is disgusting.

4

This film is scary!

5

I haven't got any money.

6

I can't see very well.

7

I love Zac Efron!

6

Choose or invent a problem. Ask your classmates for advice.

> I want to be an actor.

> I want to improve my English.

> I never remember to do my homework.

> I want to learn to swim.

> I always feel tired.

> My little sister breaks all my things.

> I want to meet new friends.

> I want to be healthier.

A I want to learn to swim. What should I do?
B You should have swimming lessons.
C You shouldn't be scared. Swimming's fun!

Imperative

7

○ 2.30 Listen and complete the text.

THE GOOD GUIDE TO EMAILS – 8 RULES

1 _____ emails as quickly as possible. (answer)

2 _____ to emails from strangers. (reply)

3 _____ a clear subject for the email. (write)

4 _____ your email with a greeting such as *Hi*, or *Dear ...* (start)

5 _____ CAPITAL letters – it's rude. (use)

6 _____ a friend's email without permission. (forward)

7 _____ your spelling and punctuation. (check)

8 _____ the email before you send it. (read)

➤ Language check page 130

Adjectives with -ed / -ing

• Some adjectives have two forms: *-ing* and *-ed*. They have different meanings.
The film was **boring**. Owen was **bored**.
The journey was **tiring**. Holly was **tired**.

8

Complete the sentences with the correct adjective.

irritated / irritating

1 The clock made an _____ noise.
Holly was _____ .

embarrassed / embarrassing

2 Owen was _____ .
His dad was very _____ .

interested / interesting

3 Holly was _____ in the book.
The book was _____ .

relaxed / relaxing

4 The music on Owen's mp3 was _____ .
He was very _____ .

depressing / depressed

5 Holly was _____ .
Her exam results were very _____ .

disgusting / disgusted

6 The food was _____ .
Owen was _____ .

Speaking and reading

1 **Warm up** Work with a partner. Ask and answer the questions.

How long do you spend on your mobile in a day?

How many text messages do you send in a day?

How fast can you text?

When do you usually text?

Where are you usually when you text?

How much money do you spend a week on your mobile?

Do you send photos to your friends and family?

Do you take videos with your mobile?

Do you text your parents? Do they text you?

THE GR8 BIG TXT FACTFILE

Can you live without your mobile?
Are you faster at texting than writing?

Do you text your friends all the time?
And what do you know about texting?

- SMS (text messages) stands for Short Messaging Service.
- The first text message was sent in 1992. It said 'Merry Christmas'.
- The busiest time for texting is between 10.30 pm and 11 pm.
- Some people send lots of texts. Andrew Acklin, 17, from Ohio, USA, sends over 20,000 messages in a month.
- Most text messages take less than 10 seconds to arrive.
- The Philippines is the texting leader of the world. People there send 1.4 billion text messages a day!

- The average US teenage texter sends approximately 80 text messages a day.
- 50% of mothers are happy to receive a text instead of a card on Mother's Day.
- In New Zealand students can use text abbreviations in their school exams!
- You can draw an emoticon of Homer Simpson! ~(_8^(|)

EMOTICONS
1 B-) cool
2 :-0 surprised
3 |-) tired
4 :-(sad
5 :"> embarrassed
6 :-) happy
7 :-/ confused
8 :'(crying

2 **Read the factfile on page 66 and answer the questions.**

1 What did the first-ever text message say?
2 How many texts does Andrew Acklin send?
3 How long does it take a text message to arrive?
4 How many texts do people in the Philippines send in a day?
5 Where can you use text abbreviations in your school exams?

3 **What do you think?**

Which information was …
• the most surprising   • the most interesting   • the funniest?

4 **Match the text abbreviations with the words and phrases. Do you use them?**

Listening

5 ⊙ **2.32 Listen and number the topics 1–3 in the order you hear them.**

homework ☐   football ☐   a party ☐

6 ⊙ **2.32 Listen to the messages again and note the missing information.**

1 Message from	Dan
Time to meet	
Place to meet	

2 Message from	
Day to meet	
Place to meet	

3 Message for	
Time of call	
Number to call	

Writing

7 **Write the text messages in complete sentences.**

Hi Sam! How are you?   Let's go and see a film today.

1 HI SAM! HOW RU? LETS GO & C A FILM 2DAY.

2 HI JOE! DO U WANT 2 C THE NEW BATMAN FILM?

3 GR8 IDEA. C U @ THE CINEMA @ 3.

4 C U L8ER.

5 HI JOE. RUOK?

6 IM FINE. WHERE R U SAM? ITS 3.15!

7 IM @ THE ABC CINEMA. WHERE R U JOE?

8 IM @ THE ODEON! LETS GO 2 C THE FILM 2MORO!

▷ Communication page 113   ▷ Your Space Web Zone   (Cyberworld   **Unit 6**   **67**)

Study skills

Speaking fluently
Don't be scared of making mistakes. It's part of learning a language!

TEXT ABBREVIATIONS

1	IC	a	before
2	CU L8ER	b	tomorrow
3	GR8	c	Are you OK?
4	LUV	d	How are you?
5	HOW R U	e	I see
6	2DAY	f	love
7	THX	g	See you later
8	2MORO	h	Great
9	RUOK	i	Thanks
10	B4	j	today

Grammar
past continuous: all forms
• adverbs of manner

Functions
talking about the past

Vocabulary • Text types

1 ⊙ **2.36** **Match the words with the pictures. Then listen and check.**

advert [7] notice [ ] note [ ] leaflet [ ] newspaper [ ] website [ ]

letter [ ] instruction manual [ ] poster [ ] magazine [ ]

2 **Work with a partner. Discuss the questions.**

Where do you find adverts / notices / posters?
What magazines / websites / newspapers do you read?
Do you ever write or receive letters / notes?

Presentation

3 **Warm up** Look at the photos on page 69. Who can you see? What are they doing?

4 ⊙ **2.37** **Listen and read Poppy's blog on page 69. Then number the photos in order.**

5 **Read Poppy's blog again and (circle) the mistakes in the sentences below. Then correct them.**

1 The friends were working at (Jack's) house. Poppy's
2 Jack and Harry were making T-shirts.
3 The team met at 9 o'clock on Sunday morning.
4 Harry called Poppy on her mobile.
5 Ricky is Alice's brother.
6 Jack was wearing his T-shirt on Sunday afternoon.

6 **Read *Language focus* and find more past continuous examples in Poppy's blog.**

7 **Find one more adverb in Poppy's blog. It is irregular.**

Language focus

• I **was writing** an advert for our website.
• The sun **was shining** this morning.
• They **were having** fun.
• I **wasn't feeling** happy.
• What **was** Jack **wearing**?

• We were working **quickly**.
• I walked **slowly** home.

My concert blog
by Poppy

A **Friday**

Our concert is only a week away. I can't believe it – scary! These are my photos! We were all at my house last night. We were working hard. And we were working quickly! Harry was printing posters. I was writing an advert for our website. Jack and Alice were designing T-shirts. They were having fun.

B **Saturday**

We met at 9 o'clock in town. Jack and Alice were wearing our new T-shirts. They looked great. Then we put up our posters for the gig. Jack and Alice were laughing all day.

In the afternoon a young guy arrived. He chatted with Alice and then they left. I said goodbye to Harry and Jack and I walked slowly home. I was tired.

C **Sunday**

The sun was shining this morning, but I wasn't feeling happy. Then Jack called me on my mobile.

'Who was Alice talking to yesterday?' I asked.

'Ricky,' said Jack.

'Is he her brother?'

'Her brother? Don't you know? Ricky's her cousin!' said Jack.

In the afternoon we practised our songs. Jack looked so cool. What was he wearing? His sunglasses, of course!

Your Space   Talking about last Saturday

8 **Write four things that you were doing at different times last Saturday. Three must be true, one must be false.**

I was watching a football match at 4 o'clock.
I was dancing at 11 o'clock at night.

9 **Look at your partner's sentences. Guess the false sentence.**

Chat zone
I can't believe it.
of course

Past continuous

1 Look at the cartoon. Complete the sentences with *was* or *were*. Use the table to help you.

	I	was	working.
	Was	I	working?
Where	was	I	working?

we / you / they	were(n't)	working
I / he / she / it	was(n't)	working

What .... Zak and Robopet doing yesterday?

The sun .... shining. It .... raining. And they .... running in the park!

2 Look at the picture and complete the sentences with the past continuous. Then write the names in the boxes.

What were the friends doing at 5 o'clock?

1 Idris .....was watching.. TV. (watch)
2 Jasmine and Eric .... to music. (listen)
3 Emma .... a magazine. (read)
4 Chloe and Eve .... table tennis. (play)
5 James .... his homework. (do)

Get it right!

Remember to use the verb *be* with the past continuous:
I was waiting for the bus when I saw the teacher. NOT ~~I waiting for the bus when I saw the teacher.~~

3 ✎ **Write negative sentences about the friends in Exercise 2.**

James / download music

Jasmine and Eric / play a video game

Idris / talk on his mobile

Emma / write a story

Chloe and Eve / chat

James wasn't downloading music.

4 ☆ **Work in pairs. How good is your memory? Cover Exercise 2. Ask and answer questions.**

A What was Idris doing?
B I think he was watching TV.
A Was Emma doing her homework?
B No, she wasn't. She was reading a magazine.

5 Complete the conversations.

A

Police officer Where were you at 2 o'clock on Sunday morning?

Harry I ¹ *was sitting* in my flat. (sit)

Police officer What ² _____ ? (you / do)

Harry I ³ _____ a film. (watch)

Police officer Were you alone?

Harry No. I was with my mate Johnny.

Police officer What film ⁴ _____ ? (you / watch)

Harry *Star Wars*. I love science fiction films.

B

Police officer Where were you at 2 am?

Johnny I was at Harry's flat.

Police officer Were ⁵ _____ the web? (you and Harry / surf)

Johnny No, we ⁶ _____ , and we ⁷ _____ computer games. (not play) We ⁸ _____ a film. (watch)

Police officer ⁹ _____ *Star Wars*? (you / watch)

Johnny No, we ¹⁰ _____ . I hate science fiction films. It was *Shrek*.

6 ○ 2.38 Listen and check.

7 ☆ Work in pairs. Act out the conversations.

8 ☆ Work in pairs. Ask and answer the questions.

> What were you doing yesterday at 6 am / 10 am / 1 pm / 4 pm / 8 pm / 11 pm ?

> I was … doing my homework / sending text messages / watching TV, etc.

> What were you wearing on Saturday / yesterday?

> I was wearing … a T-shirt / jeans / a skirt / trainers, etc.

Adverbs of manner

Adjective	Regular adverbs	Spelling rule
quick → quickly careful → carefully		add *ly*
happy → happily		*y > i + ly*

Irregular adverbs		
fast	→	fast
good	→	well
hard	→	hard

9 Complete the sentences with an adverb.

1 Don't play your music so *loudly* ! (loud)
2 I think Joe plays tennis _____ . (good)
3 Rebecca eats _____ . She never has fast food. (healthy)
4 The children played _____ . (happy)
5 George is a bit sad today. He did _____ in his exams. (bad)

10 ○ 2.39 Listen and decide how the people were talking.

She was talking slowly.

11 ☆ Work in pairs. Take turns to say the sentence in different ways (e.g. quietly, fast, slowly). Guess the adverb.

A I was walking on the beach on Sunday afternoon.
B Quietly.

7B She was talking on the phone when ...

Grammar
past continuous v. past simple
with *when* • *a/an* and *the*

Functions
talking about the past

Vocabulary • Verbs

1 ⊙ 2.40 **Match the words with the pictures. Then listen and check.**

drop ☐   lift ☐   crash 1   break ☐   catch ☐   destroy ☐   hit ☐   fall ☐

2 **Work with a partner. Answer the questions.**

Can you remember the last thing you dropped / caught / broke / hit?

Presentation

3 **Warm up** Look at the cartoons on page 73. What do you think happened?

4 **Quickly read the stories and match them with the headings below. There is one extra heading.**

1 The lucky cat of Detroit   2 **The burglar's mother**
3 A long conversation   4 **This isn't a car park!**

5 ⊙ 2.41 **Read and listen to the stories again and answer the questions.**

1 Where was Lily Foster sitting? What was she doing?
2 Why did she get up from her chair?
3 Why did the old woman wake up?
4 What did she do when she saw the burglar?
5 What were the woman and her cat doing?
6 How many times did Jamie catch the cat?

6 **Can you remember the stories? Read *Language focus*. Then complete the sentences.**

1 Lily _was watching_ (watch) TV when the phone _rang_ (ring).
2 Lily .... (talk) on the phone when a truck .... (crash) into her house.
3 An old woman .... (sleep) when she .... (hear) a noise.
4 The burglar .... (sleep) when she .... (call) the police.
5 A woman .... (play) with her cat when it .... (fall) out of the window.
6 Jamie .... walking in the street when the cat .... (land) on him.

> **Language focus**
> • Lily Foster was watching TV **when** her phone rang.
> • She was showing him her family photos **when** he fell asleep.

Strange but true!

The world is a very strange place. Read these amazing true stories.

☐ Lily Foster was watching TV when her phone rang. She got up from her chair and answered the phone in the next room. She was talking on the phone when a lorry crashed into her house. The lorry destroyed her sitting room, her TV, and her chair! And the phone call? It was a wrong number!

☐ An old woman was sleeping in her apartment in San Francisco when she heard the sound of breaking glass. She walked into her living room and saw a burglar. They were both very surprised! The 73-year-old woman offered the burglar food and then they started chatting. She was showing him her family photos when he fell asleep. So what did she do next? She called the police!

☐ A woman was playing with her cat in her apartment when it fell out of the window. Jamie Baldwin was walking in the street below when the cat landed on him – and it was safe! But that wasn't the end of the story. One year later, Jamie was walking along the same street in Detroit when he heard a noise. He looked up ... and he caught the same cat!

Write to us with your amazing stories.

Your Space   Talking about events in the past

7   **Imagine the situation. Yesterday evening at 8 pm, you were on the internet when there was a power cut. No electricity! What do you think the people below were doing? Write your ideas.**

your best friend   your neighbour   your grandparents   Spike (a burglar)
Ricky (a rock singer)   Katie (a teacher)   Lucy (a chef)   Keira (an actor)

My best friend was writing a text message.

8   **Work in pairs. Compare your ideas. Did you imagine the same things?**

Past simple v. past continuous

1 Complete the cartoon with these verbs. Use the timeline to help you.

> saw   was walking

Past continuous → Past simple

I was talking when I got a text message.

Robopet .... along the road when he .... a Robocat!

2 ⊙ 2.42 Listen and label the people in the picture.

> 1 Jeff   2 Kim   3 Joe   4 Ricky
> 5 Tom   6 Sara and Mary   7 Ella
> 8 Jim and Tim   9 Molly

3 Complete the magazine article with the verbs below.

> row a boat   do yoga   fly a kite   jog
> paint a picture   kick a football
> take a photo   play chess

The balloon in the park!

On Saturday at quarter past three, all the people in Ruskin Park got a big surprise. Jeff .... when the hot-air balloon landed. But what were other people doing? Joe and Kim ...., Ricky .... and Tom .... Sara and Mary .... when they saw the balloon, Ella ...., Jim and Tim .... and Molly .... It was a crazy afternoon!

Soundbite

/æ/ /ɑː/

a ⊙ 2.43 Listen and repeat.
1 actor accident apple crash dragon
2 car artist army nasty archer

b ⊙ 2.44 Listen and complete the table.
carrot afternoon bag can't happy partner father piano

/æ/	/ɑː/

Articles: *a / an* and *the*

The sun was shining. I was walking along **the** street when **a** dog ran out of **a** butcher's shop. **The** dog was holding **a** bone!

We use:

- *a/an* to talk about a noun for the first time: … *when **a** dog ran out …*
- *the* before a noun which you introduced before: … ***the** dog was holding …*
- *the* when there is only one of a thing: ***the** sun*
- *a/an* to refer generally to a place or thing: ***a** butcher's shop*, ***a** bone*.

4 **Complete the sentences with *a/an* or *the*.**

1   A woman and _a_ man were standing outside. _The_ woman was tall and _the_ man was short.
2   I met _____ interesting girl at Jake's party. She's _____ actor.
3   **A** Did you see _____ new English teacher yesterday?
    B I don't think so.
    A She's really nice. And she's got _____ fantastic car.
    B I didn't see her, but I saw _____ car!
4   It was _____ beautiful day.

Language check page 131

Linking words

We use *because*, *so*, *and*, *or*, *too* and *also* to link two parts of a sentence.

because / so

Jake missed the Maths test. His bus was late.
Jake missed the Maths test **because** his bus was late.
Jake's bus was late **so** he missed the Maths test.

and / or

Father: Tidy your room **and** then help me in the kitchen!
Teenager: Dad! I haven't got time. I can tidy my room **or** help you in the kitchen!

too / also

I went swimming.
I visited my gran **too**.

I went swimming.
I **also** visited my gran.

5 **Circle the correct words.**

1   Hailey's aunt gave her £20 *because /* *so* she bought a DVD.
2   They went to the cinema and they *also / too* visited a museum.
3   Do you want to go to the mountains *and / or* the seaside for our holiday?
4   I'm really hungry! Let's have pasta *and / or* a pizza!
5   Harry didn't feel well yesterday *because / so* he didn't play football.
6   I saw Ella at the party. I saw Holly *also / too*.

Reading and listening

1   **Warm up** Look at the pictures and the title of the story.
    What do you think the story is about?

2   **Read the story quickly. Were you right?**

🔊 2.46

The footprints in the snow

The snow was falling again. It was cold and the sun was sinking in the sky. Donna and Richard were walking slowly under the tall trees. They were high up the side of a hill. In the distance they could see the small town of Darksville, their destination. But they still had a long way to go before evening.

'This is a crazy time of year for a walking holiday,' said Donna.

'It's cool,' said Richard.

'Cool?' said Donna. 'It's freezing!'

And they laughed.

But a little later, they were walking through the forest when Donna saw footprints in the snow. They weren't human footprints. They were huge.

'What made these footprints?' asked Donna nervously.

'I don't know,' said Richard. 'Maybe a bear?'

Donna didn't like the idea of a bear. It worried her.

'We have to walk faster,' she said. 'I want to get to Darksville.'

It was getting dark now. Donna and Richard weren't talking. They were worrying about those footprints. They were walking round a frozen pond when Richard said, 'Look!'

Donna saw a small wooden house. But all the windows were broken and the door was destroyed. And then she saw the footprints ...

'Richard,' said Donna quietly. 'It's that thing again.'

'I don't understand,' said Richard.

'Did a yeti do this?' asked Donna.

'Yetis don't exist. Not in America.'

'Then what was it?' asked Donna. 'Bigfoot? A monster?'

'Don't be silly, Donna,' said Richard. But he was scared. And then they heard a loud sound. A human didn't make it. A bear or a wolf didn't make it. It was terrible! And Donna and Richard started to run ...

3 2.46 **Read the story again and listen. Are the sentences true (*T*) or false (*F*)?**
1 Donna and Richard were on a skiing holiday. F
2 They were walking to the town of Darksville.
3 Donna wasn't worried when she saw the footprints.
4 Richard saw the house before Donna.
5 There weren't any footprints outside the house.
6 They started running because they heard a horrible sound.

4 **What do you think? Answer the questions with a partner.**
• What made the footprints and the terrible sound?
• Do you believe creatures such as the yeti exist?

5 2.47 **Listen to the end of the story and answer the questions.**
1 Why did Donna and Richard stop running?
2 What did they hear?
3 Who was standing in the bright light?
4 What were the people doing?

Speaking

6 **Imagine you are a journalist. You are going to interview Donna and Richard. Study the questions below. Then write two more questions to ask them.**
• Where were you walking?
• What was the weather like?
• Why were the footprints scary?
• What did you see at the house?
• What did you do when you heard the loud noise?

7 **Work in pairs. One student is a journalist. The other student is Donna or Richard. Ask and answer your questions. Then swap roles.**

A Where were you walking?
B We were walking to Darksville.
 We were on holiday.

Writing

8 **Look at the picture from the latest Donna and Richard story. In groups, write the beginning of the story (about 100 words). Think about these questions.**
• Where were they?
• Why were they there?
• What were they doing?
• What happened next?

Study skills

Linking words
When you write, link your ideas with: *and, so, but*. Organise your story with these words: *First, then, after that, finally.*

8A I'm going to be a musician

Grammar
be going to: all forms

Functions
talking about future intentions

Vocabulary • Jobs

1 ◉ **3.03 Match the words with the pictures. Then listen and check.**

nurse ☐ pilot ☐ film director ☐ chef ☐ athlete ☐ musician ☐ vet ☐
firefighter ☐ scientist ☐ 1 detective ☐ engineer ☐ racing driver ☐

2 **Work in pairs.**

Which person …
works in a hospital?   plays a musical instrument?   works in a restaurant?
is very fit?   works with animals?   saves lives?   makes films?   solves mysteries?

Presentation

3 **Warm up Look quickly at the blog on page 79 and find the names of jobs.**

4 ◉ **3.04 Read and listen to the blog. Write the names.**

Who wants to …
1 travel?	**7** be a pop star?
2 cook?	**8** be a musician?
3 write a novel?	**9** work with animals?
4 compete in the Olympics?	**10** get fit?
5 save lives?	**11** be a racing driver?
6 go to drama school?	**12** be a detective?

5 **Read *Language focus* and complete the sentences.**

buy give go study ~~do~~ visit

1 I'm going to ....*do*........ a school project on Barack Obama.
2 Helena is going to .... Science at university.
3 Marco is going to .... to London at the weekend.
4 I'm going to .... Paris next year.
5 My parents aren't going to .... a new car.
6 My teacher isn't going to .... us a test.

Language focus

- **I'm going to** get fit.
- My best friend**'s going to** be a doctor.
- **I'm not going to** do a normal job.
- What **are you going to** do in the future?

It's your life.com

Home | **Blogs** | Join us

Lindsay's blog

My future plans

My best friend's going to be a doctor. My sister's going to be an artist. And I want to be a ... pop star! What are you going to do in the future?

Write to me with your answers ☺

Replies

I'm going to pass all my piano exams. And then I'm going to be a musician. *Noah*

I want to be a film director. I'm going to make my own film and show it at a film festival. *Daisy*

I'm not going to do a normal job. I'm going to be a racing driver! *Karim*

I love solving problems. I'm going to be a detective. *Rose*

First I'm going to travel round the world! But then I want to be a nurse. *Ethan*

I love animals and I love nature – it's my dream to work with them! But I'm not going to be a vet. I want to be a scientist. *Lily*

I want to be a firefighter. I'm going to get fit, so I can save lives. *Megan*

I love athletics. And I really want to compete in the Olympics. *James*

I want to be an actor. I love performing in plays. So I'm going to go to drama school. *Tristan*

I love writing! ☺ I want to be a writer. I'm going to write a mobile phone novel! It's going to be in text messages. *April*

I'm going to learn to make some really great food. I want to be a chef. *Matthew*

Your Space   Talking about future intentions

6 **Write two sentences about what you want to do in the future.**

I'm going to be an astronaut!
I'm going to study Science at university.

7 **Work in groups. Talk about your ideas.**

be going to

1 Complete the cartoons with the words below. Use the tables to help you.

| 'm | is | are | aren't |

I	'm (am)	
we / you / they	're (are)	going to read
he / she / it	's (is)	

I	'm not (am not)	
we / you / they	aren't (are not)	going to read
he / she / it	isn't (is not)	

Is she going to read?	Yes, she is. / No, she isn't.
Are you / we / they going to read?	Yes, we / you/ they are. No, we / you / they aren't.

What	is she	going to read?
	are they	

We .... going to study today!

What .... you going to do?

I .... going to play basketball. And Max .... going to paint his room!

2 Complete the sentences with the correct form of *be going to / not be going to* and the verb in brackets.

1 My grandparents haven't got any money. They <u>aren't going to go</u> on holiday. (go)
2 I didn't do very well in my exams. I .... harder next term. (study)
3 Our teacher isn't very happy here. She .... to another city. (move)
4 I .... Maths at university. I want to study English. (study)
5 They .... to the station. They've got a problem with their car. (drive)
6 You .... nervous in the exam. Geography is your best subject. (be)
7 Dylan .... some new trainers. His old ones are too small. (buy)
8 Jenny .... a big lunch. She's hungry! (have)

3 ✎ Write sentences with *be going to / not be going to* and the phrases below.

| ~~buy an mp3 player~~   learn Chinese
wear coats   use a dictionary
get up early   study this evening
watch the football match   walk slowly |

1 I haven't got much money.
  I'm not going to buy an mp3 player.
2 Nick doesn't understand the words.
  He ...
3 It's a hot day. We ...
4 The train leaves at 6 am. They ...
5 She hates sport. She ...
6 We're very early for school. We ...
7 They've got an exam tomorrow. They ...
8 Jake wants to live in Beijing. He ...

4 ⚐ **Work in pairs. Talk about your plans for the weekend.**

stay at a friend's house   help my parents   do my homework

send some text messages   tidy my room   visit relatives   watch TV

relax   hang out with friends   go swimming   stay in bed late

A What are you going to do at the weekend?
B I'm going to relax.
A Are you going to do your homework?
B No, I'm not!

5 ◯ **3.05** **Listen and match the students with the information. Draw lines.**

Emily

Josh

Olivia

Theo

Nick

loves animals   likes Maths

is good at Art   likes flying

likes writing stories

be a writer   be a vet

go to art school

work in a bank   be a pilot

Soundbite

/gənə/

◯ **3.06** **Listen and repeat the chant.**

Holly's going to act in Hollywood,
Johnny's going to climb the highest peak,
My friends are going to see the world,
But I'm going to stay in bed and sleep!

Laura's going to write a famous novel,
Harry's going to play for a football team,
My friends are going to change the world,
But I'm going to stay in bed and dream!

6 ⚐ **Work in pairs. Ask and answer questions about the people in Exercise 5.**

A What is Emily going to do?
B She's going to be a writer.
A Why is she going to be a writer?
B She likes writing stories.

7 ⚐ **Ask and answer about yourselves.**

A What are you going to do in the future / when you leave school?
B I'm going to …

8 ✎ **Write sentences about your partner.**

Pablo's going to be a doctor.

Grammar
be going to for prediction
• prepositions of movement
Functions
talking about music

Vocabulary • Musical instruments

1 ○ **3.07** **Match the words with the pictures. Then listen and check.**

electric guitar ☐   violin ☐   piano ☐   drums ☐   flute ☐
cello ☐   keyboard ☐   trumpet ☐   saxophone ☐   recorder ☐

2 ○ **3.08** **Listen and name the six instruments you hear.**

3 **Work in pairs. Answer the questions.**

• Which instruments do you blow?   • Which instruments have got strings?

Presentation

4 **Warm up** **Look at the photos on page 83 and answer the questions.**

1 Where are the friends in picture A? How do you think Poppy and Alice feel?
2 Which instruments are they playing in picture C? Who is singing?

5 ○ **3.09** **Listen and read the photo story on page 83. Are the sentences true (*T*) or false (*F*)?**

1 The friends are doing the concert to raise money. *T*
2 Poppy feels excited about the concert.
3 Poppy is worried about the weather.
4 Alice isn't worried about the concert.
5 Jack is worried because Harry isn't a good drummer.
6 There are a lot of people in the school.

6 **Read *Language focus*. Who says these sentences in the photo story?**

1 It's going to rain. Poppy
2 The concert's going to be fantastic!
3 People aren't going to come to the concert.
4 We're going to have a small audience.
5 It's going to be a nightmare!
6 It's going to fall!

Language focus

• Look at all those black clouds. It's **going to** rain.
• Harry isn't here. He's **going to** be late.

A ○ **3.09** **It's the evening of the charity concert – but Poppy is very quiet.**

Alice Are you OK, Poppy?

Poppy I feel a bit nervous.

Alice Don't worry about it. We've got good songs. You've got a great voice. The concert's going to be fantastic!

Poppy I guess so. But look at all those black clouds. It's going to rain. So people aren't going to come to the concert. We're going to have a small audience. And …

Jack Hang on. We've got a bigger problem.

Alice What is it, Jack?

Jack Harry isn't here. He's going to be late. The concert's going to start in five minutes and we haven't got a drummer. It's going to be a nightmare!

Alice You guys are terrible! Chill out!

B **Harry walks into the room … just in time!**

Harry Hi, gang!

Jack Harry! At last!

Harry I'm so excited! There are lots of people in the school! This is going to be great!

Poppy Watch that glass, Harry! It's going to fall!

Harry No worries! I've got it!

AFRICA CHALLENGE

C **The concert is a big success. The friends raise a lot of money for the Africa Challenge. And they have a great time, too!**

Your Space   Talking about music

7 **Work in groups. Ask and answer the questions. You can invent more questions.**

Do you play any musical instruments?
What's your favourite instrument?
Have you got a favourite singer or band?
What kind of music do you like?
What's the last song you listened to?

Do you play any musical instruments?
Yes, I do. I play the guitar.

Chat zone

I guess so.
Hang on.
It's going to be a nightmare!
No worries!

be going to for prediction

We're going to crash!

- Use *going to* for predictions based on something we can see in the present.

1 **What is going to happen in the pictures? Write sentences using these verbs.**

> fall in   answer   ~~fall off~~   make   have

1  The books *are going to fall off* the shelf.

2  She .... a pizza.

3  Ruth .... the phone.

4  Naomi .... a bath.

5  Tyler .... the swimming pool.

2 ✐ **Complete the sentences with your own ideas.**

1 I've got toothache. I'm *going to go to the dentist.*
2 It's a lovely day. We ...
3 I need some stamps. I ...
4 I'm tired. I ...
5 I'm hungry. I ...
6 This T-shirt is dirty. I ...

Prepositions of movement – up, down, into, out of, over, under

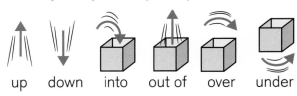

up   down   into   out of   over   under

3 **Look at the pictures and complete the sentences with the correct prepositions.**

1  Ross is going *under* the bridge.

2  Amber is skateboarding .... the hill.

3  Craig is jumping .... the wall.

4  Laura's getting .... the car.

5  Lee is coming .... his bedroom.

6  Emma is walking .... the hill.

4 **Look at the picture on page 85. Match sentences 1–6 with pictures A–F.**

1 An ice cream van is going **under** the bridge. F
2 A man is falling **into** the lake.
3 A train is coming **out of** the tunnel.
4 A boy and a girl are running **over** the bridge.
5 A girl is coming **down** the slide.
6 A girl is climbing **up** the wall.

High Top Adventure Park

Fun for all the family!

5 **Now complete these sentences with the prepositions from Exercise 3.**

1 A man is stepping _into_ a boat.
2 A girl is climbing .... the wall.
3 Two children are going .... Magic World.
4 An old lady is standing .... an umbrella.
5 A man is falling .... the lake.
6 Two children are running .... the bridge.
7 A train is coming .... the tunnel.
8 An ice cream van is going .... the bridge.

Get it right!

Use the correct preposition!

A man is stepping **out of** a boat.

NOT ~~A man is stepping out a boat.~~

Language check page 131

get

get up

Maddy always **gets up** late!

get a bus

So she doesn't always **get the bus** to school.

get to school

And she often **gets to school** late.

get a new bike

So her parents **get her a new bike**!

get tired

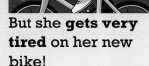

But she **gets very tired** on her new bike!

get fit

So she decides to **get fit**.

get hot

She **gets very hot** at the gym.

get better

Maddy **gets better** at sport. She gets fit. And she gets to school on time!

6 **Match the two parts of the sentences.**

1 I get up
2 I'm in the football team because
3 I get
4 My family like walking but I
5 I learn ten new words a day

a and I'm getting better at English.
b early every morning.
c get tired!
d I want to get fit.
e the train to school.

Reading

1   Warm up Look at the headline and the photo. Answer the questions.

- Who usually wears red noses?
- What are the people in the photo doing?
- What do you think Red Nose Day is?

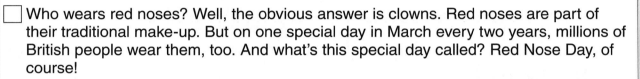

RED NOSE DAY

☐ Who wears red noses? Well, the obvious answer is clowns. Red noses are part of their traditional make-up. But on one special day in March every two years, millions of British people wear them, too. And what's this special day called? Red Nose Day, of course!

☐ On Red Nose Day, you can help people and have great fun, too. People all over the country buy millions of plastic red noses – and all the money goes to charity. Children and teenagers wear them to school and university. Even adults wear them to work! Most schools have special Red Nose Day events. Last year some students in Oxford wore pyjamas all day at school. And in a school in Cambridge, students dressed as superheroes.

☐ In a special TV programme, celebrities and comedians do silly things and viewers phone in and pay money. In 2011 people gave more than £74 million in a single day. The Prime Minister, Take That and Susan Boyle were on the show. One year, a group of celebrities, including pop stars, climbed Mount Kilimanjaro in Tanzania to raise money.

☐ An organisation called Comic Relief started Red Nose Day in 1985. A group of comedians decided to use comedy and laughter to educate people about poverty

in the UK and Africa. Its first TV programme was on Christmas Day on the BBC.

The grand total raised for charity since Comic Relief began is over £650 million! 60 per cent goes to charities in Africa and 40 per cent to charities in the UK. The money helps poor families, the old and the sick. It also helps young people to get a better education.

2 **Read the article on page 86 and match the headings with the paragraphs.**

A An amazing TV programme

B The history of Red Nose Day

C Red noses aren't only for clowns

D Red Nose Day is for everyone

3 **Read the article again and answer the questions.**

1 When does Red Nose Day happen?
2 What did students in Oxford and Cambridge do?
3 How much did Red Nose Day raise in 24 hours in 2011?
4 Who climbed Mount Kilimanjaro? Why?
5 When did Red Nose Day begin?
6 Where does the money go?

Listening and speaking

4 **○ 3.11** **Listen and draw lines between the people and the events.**

RED N●SE DAY activities

	name	last year	this year
1	Lucy	did a sponsored fancy-dress run	have a barbecue
2	Nick	did a sponsored silence	swim in pyjamas
3	Phoebe	sold cakes and biscuits	have a talent show
4	Joe	had a 'no uniform' day	have a 'red hair' day

Study skills

Listening for information
You don't have to understand every word. In Exercise 4 listen for the speakers and the activities.

5 **Work in groups. Brainstorm more ideas to raise money.**

have a joke contest
sell handmade cards

6 **Discuss the questions in groups.**

• What are the best ideas?
• Choose an idea for Red Nose Day and tell the class.

Writing

7 **Imagine you are one of the students in Exercise 4.**
Write an email to a British friend about Red Nose Day.

• Start: Hi! How are you?
• Write about what you did last year. Last year I was ...
• Give an opinion about the activity. It was ...
• Write about what you are going to do this year. This year I'm going to ...
• Finish: What are you going to do?

9A People will live on the Moon

Grammar
will for prediction

Functions
talking about the future

Vocabulary • The solar system

1 ⊙ **3.14** Do the planet puzzle. Read the clues and label the planets.
Then listen and check.

Mercury is nearest the Sun.
Venus is between Mercury and the Earth.
Pluto, a dwarf planet, is the furthest from the Sun.
Jupiter is the largest planet.

Mars is nearer to the Sun than Jupiter.
Neptune is between Pluto and Uranus.
Saturn is the second largest planet.
Uranus is next to Saturn.

2 Mercury

Presentation

2 **Warm up** Quickly read the blogs on page 89 and match the topics with the
paragraphs.

1 Education e **2** Space ☐ **3** Homes ☐ **4** Transport ☐ **5** The Environment ☐

3 ⊙ **3.15** Read and listen to the blogs again. Write the names.
Who … ?
1 … thinks holidays in space are a good idea? Brandon
2 … thinks time travel is exciting? ....
3 … is doing a school project? ....
4 … thinks computers will control houses in the future? ....
5 … thinks pollution is a big problem? ....
6 … thinks students will study at home, not at school? ....

4 Read *Language focus*. Find other examples of *will* or *won't* in the blogs.

5 Complete the predictions from the blogs with *will* or *won't*.
1 Robots will................ vacuum the floor and wash the dishes.
2 People .... drive cars with petrol.
3 People .... travel in time.
4 People .... go on holiday in space.
5 Life .... be easy for most people.
6 Students .... have homework.

6 Tick (✓) the predictions you agree with, cross (✗)
the ones you disagree with.

Language focus

- People **will live** in 'smart' houses.
- There **won't be** any schools.
- **Will** life **be** different in 100 years?
- **Yes**, it **will**.
- **No**, it **won't**.

Life in 2100

Hi there! Can you help me? I'm doing a project at school. The title? 'Will life be better in 2100?' What do you think? Thanks for your ideas, gang!

Josh

3.15

💬 Comments

a Hi Josh! I think life will be great. People will live in 'smart houses'. A central computer will control the temperature, the lights, everything!
These houses will be ecological and use solar energy and recycled water. A 'smart' mirror in the bathroom (that's right, it's a mirror with a computer!) will check your health. And guess what? Robots will cook and do the housework. *Maya*

b Pollution is a big problem today, but will be a bigger problem in 100 years. So people won't use cars with petrol. They will drive in electric cars on underground roads. And there will be electric buses with computers for drivers! The best thing? People will be able to travel in time. Now that will be exciting! *Rosie*

c Hi Josh. Life will be better in 2100 – in space! People will live on the Moon and Mars in special cities. They will grow food and send it to the Earth in a huge space craft. Space stations will orbit the Earth and control the climate. There will also be holidays in space! How cool is that? *Brandon*

d Will life be different in 100 years? Yes, it will. Will life be better? No, it won't! Climate change will cause floods and droughts. Rich people will live for a long time, maybe 200 years! But life won't be easy for most people. They won't have food and water. *Faith*

e Well, Josh, the good news is ... there won't be any schools! Students will have lessons at home on their computers. They'll be in contact with other students all over the world in a 'virtual' classroom. The bad news is ... teachers will still give us homework in the future! *Elliot*

Your Space   Talking about the future

7 (Circle) the correct words for you.

In ten years' time …
- I *will / won't* go to university.
- Astronauts *will / won't* travel to Mars.
- I *will / won't* live in a different town.
- Our national football team *will / won't* win the World Cup.
- I *will / won't* get married.

8 Compare your ideas in groups.

I'll go to university in ten years' time.

will – positive and negative

1 **Complete the cartoon. Use the table to help you.**

I / you he / she / it we / you / they	'll (will)	go

I / you he / she / it we / you / they	won't (will not)	go

In the future I .... live on a blue planet with my friends. We .... play computer games all day. We .... work!

And I .... have a beautiful wife!

2 ◉ **3.16** Listen and (circle) the correct predictions for Sophie and Adam.

⚫⚫⚫	Learn your future!	

Discover Your Future.com

Where will you be in the year 2030?
Enter your name and date of birth
and discover your future!

Name	Sophie	Adam
Date of birth	10th June 2001	6th December 2000
Job	scientist / actor	doctor / detective
Married	yes / no	yes / no
Children	1 / 2	0 / 3
City	Paris / Berlin	Los Angeles / Rio de Janeiro
Sport	running / swimming	football / tennis

3 ◉ **3.16** Listen again. Are the sentences true (*T*) or false (*F*)? Correct the false sentences.

1 Sophie will be an actor. ☐F
   Sophie won't be an actor. She'll be a scientist.
2 Adam won't be a detective. ☐
3 Sophie will get married. ☐
4 Adam won't have three children. ☐
5 Sophie will live in Paris. ☐
6 Adam will live in Rio de Janeiro. ☐
7 Sophie will go swimming in her free time. ☐
8 Adam won't play football in his free time. ☐

will – questions and short answers

4 Study the table and write questions and short answers about Sophie and Adam. Then ask and answer in pairs.

| Will | I / you
he / she / it
we / they | go? |

| Yes, | I / you / he / she / | will. |
| No, | it / we / they | won't. |

5  **Work in pairs. Ask and answer questions from Exercise 4.**

A Will Sophie be an actor?
B No, she won't.

6 Complete the conversation with the correct future form.

Ben What do you think?
¹ <u>Will life be</u> (life / be) very different in 100 years?
Lily Yes, I think cities ² _____ (be) more crowded. People ³ _____ (have) less space to live in.
Ben How ⁴ _____ (people / travel) ?
Lily They ⁵ _____ (not use) cars. They ⁶ _____ (fly) in electric flying machines!
Ben What do you think school will be like?
Lily Well, I think teachers ⁷ _____ (not be) human beings.
Ben Really? What ⁸ _____ (they / be) ?
Lily They ⁹ _____ (be) robots!

7 Write questions to ask your partner about the future.

1 go to university
1 <u>Will you go to university?</u>
2 your family move house
3 get married
4 learn to drive
5 go on holiday to the USA
6 have children
7 be famous
8 live in another country

8 Work in pairs. Ask and answer your questions from Exercise 7.

A Will you go to university one day?
B Yes, I will.

Get it right!

Use *will* to make predictions about the future.
In 100 years, people will drive electric cars. NOT ~~In 100 years, people drive electric cars.~~

9 Write sentences with *will / won't*, *may / might* or *may not / might not*.

1 we / go the theme park on Saturday (✗ not certain)
We may / might not go to the theme park on Saturday.
2 The weather / be nice tomorrow (✗ certain)
3 Freya / arrive late at the party (✓ certain)
4 We / go on holiday this year (✗ not certain)
5 Our teacher / give us a lot of homework (✗ certain)
6 I / get a lot of birthday cards this year (✓ not certain)

Grammar
first conditional

Functions
talking about technology

Vocabulary • Computer verbs

1 ◉ **3.17** (Circle) the correct verbs.
Listen and check.

1 Don't (delete)/ *turn off* that file!
   It's important!
2 I'm going to *download /*
   press some new songs.
3 Can you *delete / connect* the
   camera to the computer, please?
4 Don't *turn off / scroll* the
   computer! I want to use it.
5 *Save / Scroll* down the document.
   The information we need is at the bottom.
6 Now *turn off / click on* that icon.
7 I have to *turn off / open* a new folder.
8 Can you *print / connect* that document?
   I want to read it on the bus.
9 You must remember to *delete / save*
   your work every 15 minutes.

Presentation

2 **Warm up Look at the photos on page 93 and discuss the questions.**

- Where are the friends?
- What do you think they are doing?
- What is Jack's problem?

3 ◉ **3.18** **Listen and read the photo story on page 93. Are the sentences**
true (*T*) or false (*F*)?

1 They are making a website about the Africa Challenge. T
2 They are using Poppy's computer.
3 Poppy tries to help Jack.
4 Alice tells them all to calm down.
5 Poppy will finish the website more quickly than Jack.
6 Jack's mum will make some pizzas.

Language focus

- **If** you **restart** your computer, it**'ll** work better.
- **If** you **hit** the computer, you**'ll** break it!

4 **Read *Language focus*. Then match the beginnings**
and ends of the sentences from the photo story.

1 If we put that photo on the website,   a she'll make some popcorn.
2 If we click here,   b if I do the website.
3 If we argue,   c it'll take us to the new webpage.
4 We'll finish sooner   d it'll be really funny.
5 If I ask my mum,   e we won't finish the website.

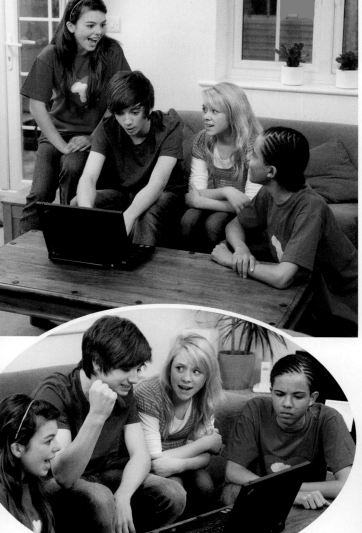

A **3.18** **It's Saturday afternoon and the team are making an Africa Challenge website.**

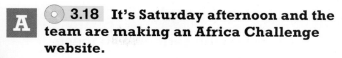

Alice	We can put all our photos on the website.
Harry	Yeah, the photos of the concert and the nature garden …
Alice	And I've got a brilliant photo of you and your bike, Harry. If we put that photo on the website, it'll be really funny!
Harry	No, it won't!
Jack	I don't get it. My computer's really slow today.
Poppy	If you restart your computer, it'll work better.
Jack	Good idea. Come on! Come on! …

B **Jack is having problems with the website …**

Jack	OK … we're connecting to the internet again. Oh no! Where's my new webpage? I didn't save it.
Poppy	Jack! If you hit the computer, you'll break it!
Jack	Have you got a better idea?
Poppy	Yes, I have. If we click here, it'll take us to the new webpage.
Jack	Very clever!
Alice	Hey! Chill out! If we argue, we'll never finish the website!

C **Jack makes a confession.**

Jack	You know … I don't really like computers.
Poppy	Really? I love them! So let me do it. We'll finish sooner if I do the website.
Alice	And then we can go for a pizza!
Jack	Great!
Harry	I'm hungry now.
Jack	If I ask my mum, she'll make us some popcorn.
Harry	Hurray!

Your Space   Talking about technology

5 **Work with a partner. Plan a new website for your school. Think about these things.**

- what you will call it
- what pictures you will put on it
- what the different sections will be, e.g. home page, sport, map, classrooms, homework

Chat zone
I don't get it!
Come on!
Very clever!

First conditional

1 Complete the cartoon with these verbs. Use the table to help you.

go   see

If we .... to New York, we'............ .... Zak's family!

If I **go** to Egypt,	I**'ll visit** the Pyramids.
If Zoe **runs** the race,	she **won't** win.

2 Complete the sentences with the correct form of the verb in brackets.

1 They won't travel tomorrow if it _snows._ (snow)
2 If David goes to the park, I .... him there. (meet)
3 You won't get to the party if you .... the bus. (miss)
4 If you press save now, you .... the information. (not lose)
5 If I .... late for the lesson, my teacher will be annoyed. (be)
6 If my parents buy me a new guitar, I .... it every day. (play)

3 ✎ Write the sentences.

1 If / Julia invite me to her party / I go
   If Julia invites me to her party, I'll go.
2 If / it not rain / we play tennis
3 If / you not leave now / you miss the bus
4 If / you read this book / you love it
5 If / I save enough money / I buy some new speakers
6 If / Jake buy a new mp3 player / he give me his old one

4 🔊 **3.19** Listen and tick (✓) the correct picture.

1 If I get a good job, …

2 If we go on holiday this year, …

3 If Joe passes his exams, …

4 If my sister learns Spanish, …

Madrid ☐   Buenos Aires ☐

5 If I get married, …

6 If my dad learns to play a musical instrument, …

5 ✎ **Write the complete sentences for Exercise 4.**

1 If I get a good job, I'll buy a big house.

First conditional questions

6 **Study the tables. Then write questions and short answers.**

What film	will you watch	if you go to the cinema?
Will you play football		if you go to the park?

Yes,	I / you / he / she / it / we / they	will.

No,	I / you / he / she / it / we / they	won't.

1 you play video games / you stay at home (✓)
   Will you play video games if you stay at home? *Yes, we will.*
2 you watch an action film / you go to the cinema (✗)
3 Isabella study Science / she go to university (✓)
4 they visit New York / they go to America (✗)
5 your mum be angry / we listen to loud music (✗)

7 **Put the words in the correct order to make questions.**

1 you go to bed late / will you feel / if / how / ?
   How will you feel if you go to bed late?
2 if / will you do / you don't feel well tomorrow / what / ?
3 will you go / where / it rains this afternoon / if / ?
4 what / if / you go shopping / will you buy / ?
5 you go to / what / will you do / if / your local town centre / ?

8 ☆ **Work in pairs. Ask and answer the questions in Exercise 7.**

A How will you feel if you go to bed late?
B I'll feel terrible!

⇨ **Language check page 132**

Compound nouns

Compound nouns have two parts: noun + noun or adjective + noun. Some compound nouns become one word, others stay as two words.

9 **Match the words to make compound nouns.**

1 lap	**a** board
2 pass	**b** console
3 white	**c** mat
4 remote	**d** top
5 games	**e** saver
6 mouse	**f** control
7 screen	**g** word
8 key	**h** board

10 **Label the pictures with the compound nouns from Exercise 9.**

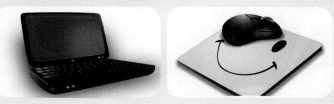

1 ....   5 ....

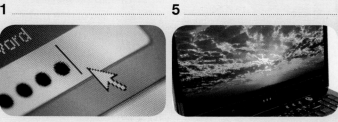

2 ....   6 ....

3 ....   7 ....

4 ....   8 ....

11 **Work in groups. What other compound nouns do you know?**

Reading

1   Look at the photos. Do you recognise the robots? Do you know any other robots in films or books?

ROBOT WORLD

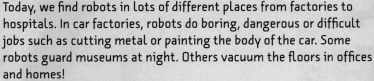

WHAT DO YOU THINK OF WHEN YOU SEE THE WORD 'ROBOTS'? SCIENCE-FICTION METAL MONSTERS OR MACHINES THAT LOOK LIKE PEOPLE? ROBOTS ARE ALL AROUND US TODAY AND THEY DO A LOT OF DIFFERENT THINGS.

Karel Capek, a Czech writer, used the word 'robot' for the first time in 1921. It comes from the Czech word *robota*. In his play 'R.U.R.'(Rossum's Universal Robots), a factory makes robots. Unfortunately, the robots kill all the humans and control the world! It's a scary story.

Today, we find robots in lots of different places from factories to hospitals. In car factories, robots do boring, dangerous or difficult jobs such as cutting metal or painting the body of the car. Some robots guard museums at night. Others vacuum the floors in offices and homes!

These robots don't look like people, but they are similar. In humans, the brain sends messages to different parts of the body and controls its movements. In robot technology, a main computer controls the movements of the robot in the same way.

Robots are very useful for exploring space. Russian robots walked on the Moon in the 1970s, and the Americans landed two robots on Mars in 2004. But why send robots into space? Well, robots can go to places that are dangerous for humans. They don't need oxygen or food and drink, and they can survive extreme temperatures. In space this is important. Temperatures can go from 120°c in the sun to −100°c in the dark!

These days, the most advanced robots can hear, see and make decisions. They have AI or 'artificial intelligence'. In the future, we will use robots in many more different ways. Doctors will use very small robots called nanobots to treat illnesses. They are so small that you can't see them!

2 Read the article and answer the questions.

1 When did Karel Capek invent the word 'robot'?
2 Where does the article say we can find robots today?
3 What controls a robot's movements?
4 When did robots first go to the Moon?
5 Why are robots useful in space?
6 What can robots with AI do?

3 What does the article say robots will do in the future? What do you think they will do?

DIARY

> **Study skills**
>
> **Reading for information**
> Underline the key words in the questions.
> _When did Karel Capek invent the word 'robot'?_
> Look for the key words in the text.

Listening and speaking

4 What can you see in the picture? Why do you think the objects are important?

5 ● 3.21 Listen to the TV programme and circle the correct answers.

1 Jamie is _buying / making_ a time capsule.
2 You have to choose items that are _interesting / important_ to you.
3 It is _easy / difficult_ to make a time capsule.
4 Jamie is using a _plastic / metal_ box for his container.
5 You _can / can't_ decide when people will open the box.
6 A time capsule will show people in the _past / future_ how we live today.

6 Plan a time capsule to open in the year 2500. Write five things to put in it. Choose items that are important to you.

7 Work in pairs. Discuss your choices. Why is each object important to you?

A Why did you choose _Shrek_?
B It's my favourite film. And it's the best animation film ever!

a Shrek DVD
my mobile phone
my cap
my skateboard
my Michael Morpugo book

Writing

8 Write a letter to put in your time capsule. Write about your life and explain why you chose the five items.

- **Start**   Dear people in the year 2500
- **Write a paragraph about your life (family and home, school, interests and hobbies)**
  I live in an apartment in Prague with my family, etc.
- **Write a paragraph about the five items and why they are important to you**
  There are five things in this time capsule. I chose Shrek because ... etc.
- **Finish**   Best wishes   [Your name]

10A Have you ever ... ?

Grammar
present perfect: all forms • *never*

Functions
asking about experiences in the past

Vocabulary • Activities

1 ⊙ **3.24** **Match the words with the pictures. Then listen and check.**

score a goal [8]   swim 100 metres ☐   win a trophy ☐   ride a horse ☐
watch a cricket match ☐   climb a mountain ☐   go skiing ☐   run a marathon ☐
play badminton ☐   meet a sports star ☐

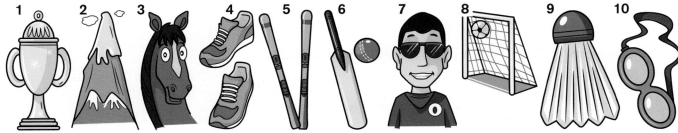

Presentation

2 **Warm up** Look at the photo story on page 99. **Where are Poppy, Alice and Jack? What are they doing?**

3 ⊙ **3.25** **Listen and read the photo story on page 99 and answer the questions.**

1 Who asks the quiz questions?
2 What does Alice think about cricket?
3 Why does Poppy ask the questions in part B?
4 Do they finish the quiz? Why / Why not?

4 **Look at *Language focus*. Then <u>underline</u> the *Have you ever ... ?* questions in the photo story.**

5 **Complete the questionnaire with the verbs below. You can use some verbs more than once.**

> met   watched   won   played   gone
> climbed   ~~scored~~   run   swum   ridden

Language focus

- **Have you ever scored** a goal?
- **Yes, I have.**
- **Have you ever won** a trophy?
- **No, I haven't.**
- **I've swum** 200 metres.
- **I haven't climbed** a mountain.

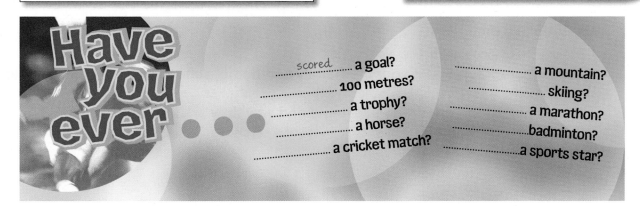

scored a goal?
.... 100 metres?
.... a trophy?
.... a horse?
.... a cricket match?
.... a mountain?
.... skiing?
.... a marathon?
.... badminton?
.... a sports star?

A 🔘 **3.25 It's lunchtime, and Poppy, Jack and Alice are relaxing on the school playing field.**

Jack Hey, this looks fun. A sports questionnaire.
Poppy Oh no, not sport.
Alice Go on then. Ask me the questions.
Jack OK. Have you ever scored a goal?
Alice Yes, I have.
Poppy Not in the park with your friends, Alice. Have you ever scored a goal in a match?
Alice Yes, I have. For the school girls' team. But only one!
Jack Have you ever swum 100 metres?
Alice Yes, I have. In fact, I've swum 200 metres!
Jack And have you ever won a trophy?
Alice No, I haven't! And I've never won a competition.
Jack Have you ever ridden a horse?
Alice Yes, I have.
Jack Have you ever watched a cricket match?
Alice No, I haven't. It's too boring.
Jack Have you ever climbed a mountain?
Alice Me? Are you joking? I've never climbed a hill!

B **Poppy asks some different questions ...**

Poppy Have you ever washed cars? Have you ever done a charity bike ride? And have you ever performed in a concert?
Jack Those questions aren't in the magazine!
Poppy I know! But we've all done them! ... Uh oh. Break's over.
Alice What a shame! It was a laugh.

Your Space **Talking about sport**

6 **In pairs, do the quiz from Jack's magazine. Answer *Yes, I have* or *No, I haven't.***

Have you ever scored a goal?
No, I haven't.

Chat zone
Go on then.
What a shame!
It was a laugh.

Present perfect – positive and negative

1 Match the sentences with the cartoons. Then complete the sentences. Use the table to help you.

In my life

I .... walked on the Moon. ☐

We .... flown in a helicopter. ☐

I .... visited Australia. ☐

subject	verb *have*	past participle
I / you	've (have)	
he / she / it	's (has)	worked.
we / they	've (have)	

subject	verb *have*	past participle
I / you	haven't (have not)	
he / she / it	hasn't (has not)	worked.
we / they	haven't (have not)	

2 Unscramble the letters to make verbs. Then match them with their past participles.

tiwer   write
keaps   ....
tea   ....
evig   ....
eb   ....
niw   ....
tmee   ....
espel   ....
ekat   ....
rahe   ....

slept
written
eaten
given
heard
been
met
won
taken
spoken

3 Complete the sentences with the past participles from Exercise 2.

1 I've never _heard_ the song of a whale.

2 My grandparents don't like travelling. They've never .... to another country.

3 Take a look at my website. I've .... an amazing story!

4 My father's a journalist and he's .... lots of famous people.

5 My uncle and aunt have .... me a fantastic birthday present.

6 Andy has .... a funny photo of his dog.

7 My sister's vegetarian. She's never .... a hamburger!

8 Tom feels very nervous. He hasn't .... in public before.

9 Guess what! I've .... under the stars in a desert!

10 Millie has .... three swimming medals.

4 ○ **3.26** **Listen to Leo talking about his amazing life. Write the missing verbs.**

THIS IS MY LIFE!

I've _____ (Angelina Jolie) / Demi Moore.
I've _____ spiders / scorpions.
I've _____ in Australia / Portugal.
I've _____ polar bears / African elephants.
I've _____ the Taj Mahal in India /
The Great Wall of China.
I've _____ in a tent / in a boat.

5 **Listen again and ⟨circle⟩ the correct experiences.**

Questions with *have you ever ...* ?

6 ✎ **Write questions with *ever* and short answers.**

1 they / go / on a skiing holiday? (✓)
   Have they ever been on a skiing holiday?
   Yes, they have.
2 you / use / an internet café? (✓)
3 Jake / visit / the Science Museum? (✗)
4 she / eat / Mexican food? (✗)
5 your grandmother / surf / the web? (✓)
6 you / study / jazz dance? (✗)
7 they / listen to / rap music? (✗)
8 Hugo / read / a book in English? (✓)

7 ✎ **Write true sentences about you.**

1 │ act in a play │
   I have / haven't acted in a play.
2 │ eat Indian food │
3 │ go to London │
4 │ ride a horse │
5 │ write a diary │
6 │ make your own website │
7 │ fly in a plane │
8 │ sleep under the stars │

8 ✉ **Work in pairs. Ask and answer questions about your experiences.**

A Have you ever acted in a play?
B Yes, I have. / No, I haven't.

Soundbite

○ **3.27** **Listen and repeat.**

Have you ever seen an elephant?
Have you ever touched a snake?
Have you ever met the president?
Have you ever baked a cake?

Have you ever acted in a play?
Have you ever eaten honey?
Have you ever slept for one whole day?
Have you ever found some money?

1 Warm up Do the Your Space quiz with a partner.

A What do you think?
B I think the answer's c.
A I agree. / I don't agree.

A I know this one. It's b.
B Are you sure?
A Yes, I'm positive.

2 ⊙ **3.28** Listen and check your answers. How many correct answers did you get?

The Your Space Quiz

It's the best general knowledge quiz ever!

1 .... is the largest desert in the world.
a The Sahara   **b** Antarctica
c The Sonoran

2 The Eiffel Tower is taller than ...
a the Empire State Building
b the Great Pyramid of Giza
c the London Eye

3 Which one of these planets is nearer the Sun than Jupiter?
a Saturn   **b** Neptune   **c** Mars

4 On 20 July 1969, Neil Armstrong was walking ...
a on the Great Wall of China
b on the bottom of the Pacific Ocean
c on the Moon

5 What does this emoticon mean?

a cool
b embarrassed
c amazed

6 Every year, people around the world use 50 billion plastic bags. That's .... bags!
a not enough   b too many   c too much

7 If you go to 1600 Pennsylvania Ave NW, Washington DC, you will see ...
a Buckingham Palace   b The White House
c Disneyland

8 How many rings are there on the official Olympic flag?
a 5   b 7   c 9

9 Which famous character did J.K. Rowling create?
a Tintin
b Harry Potter
c Frankenstein

10 What is going to happen next?
a It's going to snow.
b The concert's going to begin.
c Harry's going to arrive.

11 During extreme hot weather, you have to ...
a do lots of exercise   b drink lots of fluids
    c eat heavy food

12 Where were the 2012 Olympic Games?
a The United Kingdom
b Russia
c Germany

13 More and more people are writing blogs. But what is a blog?
a a text message
b an online diary
c a type of poem

14 In the fourteenth century, Marco Polo travelled to China from ...
a Madrid   b Venice   c Paris

15 On a social networking site, you should use ...
a short words   b emoticons   c an invented name

16 How long can a rhinoceros live?
a 25 years
b 50 years
c 100 years

Your Space   Write your own quiz

3 Work in teams. Write eight general knowledge questions or questions about Your Space 2.

What are the names of Poppy's friends?

4 Swap your questions with another team. How many correct answers can you get?

Making comparisons

1 Write the superlative form of the adjectives. Then complete the questionnaire with your own ideas.

What's the...?

		You	Your partner
most beautiful	(beautiful) place in your town?	The park	
	(small) piece of technology you own?		
	(boring) thing you do every day?		
	(funny) film you've ever seen?		
	(good) programme on TV?		
	(exciting) book you have ever read?		

2 ⭐ Work in pairs. Ask and answer questions. Note the answers.

A What's the most beautiful place in your town?

B The park.

Talking about the past

3 📖 Read the beginning of the story and write the verbs in the correct tense.

Underground adventure

It was a hot, still morning. The sun ¹was shining (shine) in a perfect blue sky and the small waves ²_____ (break) on the beach.
'This is just perfect,' said Donna.
'You are so right,' ³_____ (agree) Richard.
They ⁴_____ (walk) on the yellow sand when they ⁵_____ (hear) a strange noise.
They ⁶_____ (stop) and ⁷_____ (listen).
'What was that?' asked Donna.
Richard ⁸_____ (shake) his head. 'It seemed to come from below the beach.'
While they ⁹_____ (stand) there, they ¹⁰_____ (see) the sand move beneath their feet. A hole was forming in front of their eyes! And it ¹¹_____ (get) bigger and bigger!
They ¹²_____ (try) to get away but it was impossible. They fell into the dark, dark hole ...

4 ⭐ Work in pairs. Write the next episode of the story.

Talking about the present

5 ⭐ **Work in pairs. Put the words in order to make questions. Then ask and answer the questions.**

1 do | what time | go to bed | you | ?
What time do you go to bed?
2 a day | you | text messages | do | send | how many | ?
3 you | are | today | what | wearing | ?
4 get to school | how | you | do | ?
5 doing | are | what | at the moment | your parents | ?
6 you | do | do | how often | sport | ?

Giving advice

6 ✏️ **Write a piece of advice for each of the problems.**

1 *You should watch TV programmes in English.*

> I want to improve my English.

> I feel bored.

> I want to be an actor.

> I want to be in a band.

> I never remember to do my homework.

> My best friend is angry with me.

> My sister eats all my chocolate.

> I want to learn to swim.

> I don't understand Maths.

> I can't sleep at night.

7 **In groups, take turns to choose a problem from Exercise 6. Tell your classmates your advice. Vote for the best advice!**

A I have a problem. I'm really bored. What should I do?
B You should spend less time on the computer.
C You shouldn't watch TV all the time.
D You should go and see your friends.
A That's a great idea. Thanks!

Language check page 132

Verbs with *to*, *about*, *for*

8 🔊 **3.29 Complete these sentences with *to*, *for* or *about*. Then listen and check.**

1 Alex is thinking *about* his new bike.
2 Sam often listens .... heavy metal.

3 Andy is paying .... his lunch.
4 Izzie tells her mum .... her day at school.

Please, Dad ...

5 Oscar often asks his dad .... money.
6 This phone belongs .... her dad.

7 Josh is learning .... skateboard.
8 Megan is waiting .... the school bus.

Reading and speaking

1 **Warm up** Look at the photo and the headline in the article. Who is he? What does he do? Why is he famous?

2 Read the first paragraph and check your ideas.

The King of Speed

He is the youngest driver to win the Formula One World Championship. Who is he? Lewis Hamilton, the King of Speed!

A Lewis Hamilton was born in Stevenage, UK on 7 January 1985. His parents divorced when he was only two. He lived with his mother for his first twelve years, then he lived with his father and stepmother.

B Lewis became interested in racing when he was only six. His father bought him a radio-controlled car, and soon after, a go-kart. Lewis won his first British karting championship when he was only ten. And 10-year-old Lewis also met the McLaren team owner Ron Dennis and told him, 'I want to race in Formula 1.'

C When he was still only 13, Lewis joined the McLaren and Mercedes-Benz Young Driver Support Programme. But he did other sports, too, and played for his school football and cricket teams.

D He began his car racing career in 2001 when he joined the McLaren racing team. In his first season in Formula One in 2006, Lewis won an amazing four times. In his second season, he came second in the championship. And in 2008, when he was still only 23, he won the trophy!

E Lewis is an inspiration to young people all around the world. He has also got his own heroes, including his father, Nelson Mandela and Martin Luther King.

F In his spare time, Lewis enjoys listening to music. His favourite music is R & B, reggae and hip-hop. His favourite artists include De La Soul, 2Pac and Bob Marley. But he also likes playing the guitar, too!

G Some of his other hobbies are going to the gym, cycling and tennis. He's also got a black belt in karate! But Lewis isn't active all the time. He also loves reading, watching DVDs and hanging out with family and friends.

3 Read the article and match the questions with paragraphs A–G.

1 What music does he like? F
2 When was he born?
3 Who are his heroes?
4 What other hobbies has he got?

5 How old was he when he discovered car racing?
6 What did he join when he was 13?
7 When did he begin Formula One racing?

4 Read the article again and answer the questions.

1 What did he achieve when he was ten?
2 How many races did he win in his first Formula One season?
3 How old was he when he won the F1 World Championship?
4 What musical instrument can he play?

5 Work in pairs. Do an interview with Lewis Hamilton. Read your role cards below.

> **Student A**
> Interview Lewis Hamilton.
> You can use the questions in
> Exercises 3 and 4 for ideas.

> **Student B**
> You are Lewis Hamilton.
> Answer the questions. Try to
> remember the information!

A When were you born?
B I was born on 7 January 1985.

Listening and writing

6 ⊙ **3.31** Listen to the radio interview and complete the Factfile about Shanaze Reade.

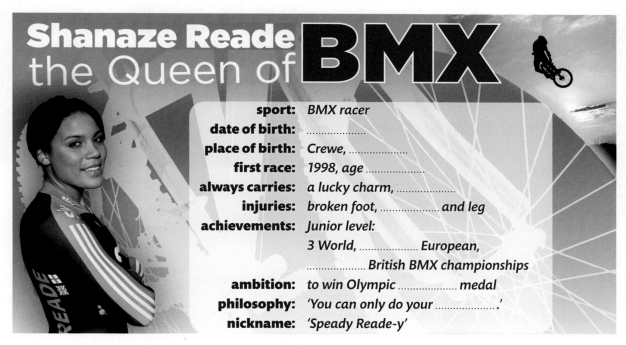

Shanaze Reade the Queen of BMX

sport:	BMX racer
date of birth:	....
place of birth:	Crewe, ...
first race:	1998, age ....
always carries:	a lucky charm, ...
injuries:	broken foot, ... and leg
achievements:	Junior level:
	3 World, ... European,
	.... British BMX championships
ambition:	to win Olympic .... medal
philosophy:	'You can only do your ....'
nickname:	'Speady Reade-y'

7 Choose a sports star and make a Factfile similar to Shanaze Reade's.

8 Write a short biography of your sports star.
  • paragraph 1: basic information (date of birth / parents / home)
  • paragraph 2: sporting achievements
  • paragraph 3: freetime activities

> **Study skills**
>
> **Doing research**
> Use reliable websites.
> Save paper! Don't print
> out information, make
> notes instead. Then use
> your notes to write your
> biography.

Classroom survival

1   Warm up **Look at the picture. Where are the students?
What is the teacher doing?**

2   ◉ **1.16** **Read the classroom conversations.
Can you guess the missing words? Listen and check.**

A   Joe   How do you say this in English?
Lucy 'Scissors'.
Joe   How do you ¹............... that?
Lucy S – C – I – S – S – O – R – S.
Joe   Can you ²............... more slowly?
Lucy Sure. It's S – C – I – S – S – O – R – S.

B   Joe   What does 'huge' mean?
Lucy Sorry, I don't ³............... .

C   Joe   Excuse me, what does 'huge'
mean?
Teacher It ⁴...............very big.

D   Teacher Lucy, do you lay the table at home?
Lucy Sorry, I don't ⁵............... .
Teacher Do you put the dishes and things
on the table before dinner?
Lucy Oh, I see. Yes, I do.

E   Teacher Do the exercises on page 65 for
homework.
Joe   Can you ⁶............... that, please?
Teacher Yes, of course. For homework, do
the exercises on page 65.
Joe   Thanks.

Phrasebook

Asking questions
What does 'huge'
mean?
How do you say this in
English?
How do you spell that?
Excuse me, can you
repeat that, please?
Can you speak more
slowly?
Answering questions
Yes, of course. / Sure.
Sorry, I don't know.

3   ◉ **1.17** **Look at *Phrasebook*. Listen and repeat.**

4   **Work in pairs. Act out the conversations in Exercise
2. Then act out new conversations. Ask about other
words in Unit 1.**

Asking for information

1 **Warm up** **Work in pairs. Choose two things to do in Cambridge.**

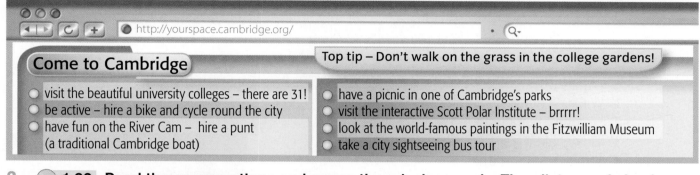

http://yourspace.cambridge.org/

Come to Cambridge

Top tip – Don't walk on the grass in the college gardens!

- visit the beautiful university colleges – there are 31!
- be active – hire a bike and cycle round the city
- have fun on the River Cam – hire a punt (a traditional Cambridge boat)

- have a picnic in one of Cambridge's parks
- visit the interactive Scott Polar Institute – brrrrr!
- look at the world-famous paintings in the Fitzwilliam Museum
- take a city sightseeing bus tour

2 **1.32** **Read the conversations and guess the missing words. Then listen and check.**

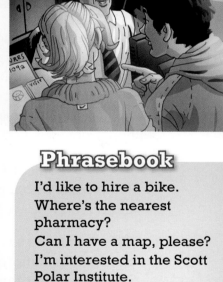

A **Man** Can I ¹_____ you?

Anna Where's the nearest Post Office?

Man There's ²_____ in St Andrew's Street. It's very close. I can show you on the map.

Anna Thanks.

B **Max** I'd ³_____ to visit the city art gallery. Is it open today?

Man Yes, it's open from 10 am until 5 pm, but it's closed on Monday.

Max Can I have a map, please?

Man Yes, of course. ⁴_____ you are.

C **Eric** I'm interested in the sightseeing bus tour. How does it work?

Man You buy a 24-hour ticket but you can get on and off the bus. For under 15-year-olds it costs £7.00. There is a commentary in different languages.

Eric Thank you very ⁵_____ .

Man No problem. Have a ⁶_____ day!

D **Carlos** Can I ⁷_____ a punting tour here?

Man Yes. You can book an official tour here. Or you can book at the punt station.

Carlos I'm sorry, I don't ⁸_____ . Do you speak Spanish?

Man Yes, a little.

Phrasebook

I'd like to hire a bike.
Where's the nearest pharmacy?
Can I have a map, please?
I'm interested in the Scott Polar Institute.
Is it open today?
Can I book a guided tour here?
How does it work?
I'm sorry, I don't understand.

3 **1.33** **Look at *Phrasebook*. Listen and repeat.**

4 **Work in pairs. Student A is a tourist and Student B is a Tourist Guide in your town or city. Ask and answer questions.**

A Where is the university?
B It's all around the city, not just in one place. There are 31 colleges!

Telling a story

1 Warm up Look at these activities. Are they part of a good day (✓) or a bad day (✗)? Tick or cross them.

forget your mobile phone ☐   have an ice cream ☐   see a football match ☐
miss a train ☐   lose your money ☐

2 ⊙ 1.44 Read and listen to the conversation. Are the sentences true (T) or false (F)?

1 Will didn't have a great day on Saturday.
2 He got a bus home.
3 Vicky called her friends on her mobile.
4 She missed the train.

Will	I had a great day on Saturday.
Vicky	Did you?
Will	I went to London with Lisa and Alex. We went to a football match. It was fun!
Vicky	What did you do next?
Will	We had an ice cream. And after that we got a taxi home.
Vicky	You lucky thing! I had a terrible day.
Will	Really?
Vicky	I went shopping. First of all, I forgot my mobile. So I couldn't call my friends.
Will	No way!
Vicky	But then I lost my money. It was terrible! Then I missed the train!
Will	Poor you!

3 ⊙ 1.45 Look at *Phrasebook*. Listen and repeat. Then work with a partner. Act out the conversation in Exercise 2.

4 Take it in turns to act out new conversations with your partner. Make notes before you start. One of you had a great day, the other had a terrible day.

• **Where?** Hollywood
• **When?** Monday
• **What?** met Kristen Stewart, had lunch

A I had a fantastic day on Monday.
B Did you?
A I went to Hollywood. And I met Kristen Stewart.
B What did you do next?
A We had lunch together.
B No way!

Phrasebook

Linking ideas
First of all ...
Then ...
After that ...
Opinions
It was terrible!
I had a great day.
Responding
No way!
Oh no!
Poor you!
Lucky you!
What did you do next?
Did you?
Really?

Shopping

1 Warm up Read the information about the museum and answer the questions.

   1 What can you see and do at the museum?

   2 When is the museum open?

2 ◉ **2.11** Read and listen to the conversation. Are the sentences true (*T*) or false (*F*)?

   1 The T-shirt is £9.   **3** Alexander buys T-shirts.

   2 The pencils are £1.50 each.   **4** Francesca spends £4.50.

Alexander	Excuse me, how much is the dinosaur T-shirt?
Shop assistant	£9.
Alexander	Right. And how much are these pencils?
Shop assistant	They're £1.50 each.
Alexander	Can I have two pencils, please?
Shop assistant	That's £3, please.
Alexander	Here you are.
Shop assistant	Thanks.
Shop assistant	Is that everything?
Francesca	Yes, thanks.
Shop assistant	So, two fridge magnets, a pencil case and two bookmarks. That's £15.50.
Francesca	Here you are.
Shop assistant	Thanks. Here's £4.50 change.
Francesca	Thanks.

Visit the

Natural History Museum

and learn all about the natural world.

It's fun. There are amazing dinosaurs and excellent exhibitions.

Investigate the fantastic science lab for 7 to 14-year-olds.

There are some great cafés!

And visit the BRILLIANT shop!

Open every day except 24 – 26 December   10 a.m. – 5.50 p.m.

3 ◉ **2.12** Look at *Phrasebook*. Listen and complete the sentences. Then listen again and repeat.

4 Work in pairs. Act out the conversation in Exercise 2. Then act out new conversations about other souvenirs in the picture.

Phrasebook

Excuse ¹_____ , how much is the fridge magnet?

How ²_____ are the key rings?

³_____ I have that soft toy, please?

Is that ⁴_____ ?

⁵_____ £6.50.

⁶_____ you are.

Here's ⁷_____ change.

Making arrangements

1 **Warm up** **Work with a partner. What might you do this weekend? Write as many different activities as you can. Then compare your ideas in groups.**

go shopping   *tidy my room*

2 **2.21** **Read and listen to the conversation. Then answer the questions.**

1 What does Jessica want to do on Saturday morning?
2 What is Liam doing on Saturday morning?
3 What do they arrange to do on Saturday afternoon?

Jessica	Hi Liam.
Liam	Oh, hi Jess.
Jessica	Would you like to go swimming on Saturday morning?
Liam	I'm sorry, I can't. I'm playing video games with Nathan.
Jessica	Don't worry. That's OK.
Liam	What are you doing on Saturday afternoon?
Jessica	Erm ... nothing.
Liam	It's my birthday! I'm going to the cinema with some friends. Would you like to come?
Jessica	Yes, I'd love to. What time?
Liam	Come to my house at three o'clock.
Jessica	Thanks. See you then!

3 **2.22** **Look at *Phrasebook*. Listen and complete. Then listen again and repeat.**

4 **Work in pairs. Act out the conversation in Exercise 2.**

5 **Fill in the diary below, then make arrangements with other students.**

A Would you like to go shopping on Saturday afternoon?
B I'm sorry, I can't. I'm playing tennis with Daniel.
A Don't worry. That's OK.

	Saturday	Sunday
morning		
afternoon		
evening		

Phrasebook

Inviting
Would you ¹_____ to go swimming on Saturday?
What are you ²_____ on Saturday afternoon?

Accepting
Yes, I'd ³_____ to. Thanks.
That's a ⁴_____ idea.

Apologising
I'm ⁵_____ , I can't.
I'm watching a DVD with Alex.

Accepting apologies
Don't worry. That's ⁶_____ .

Asking for and giving opinions

1 🔘 **2.33 Warm up Match the posters with the film types. Then listen and check.**

musicals ☒2 action films ☐ fantasy films ☐
cartoons ☐ science fiction films ☐ superhero films ☐

2 **Write the numbers of the film types (1–6) next to the films below.**

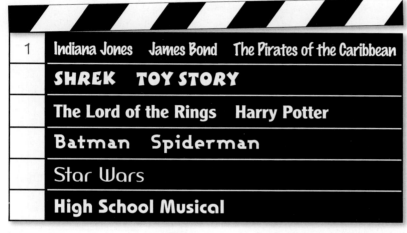

1	Indiana Jones James Bond The Pirates of the Caribbean
	SHREK TOY STORY
	The Lord of the Rings Harry Potter
	Batman Spiderman
	Star Wars
	High School Musical

3 🔘 **2.34 Listen and circle the films they talk about. Then act out the conversation.**

Lisa What films do you like?
Alex I like ¹ **action** / **fantasy** films.
Lisa Me too. Do you like ² **musicals** / **cartoons**?
Alex Yes, I do. I really like ³ **High School Musical** / **Shrek**.
Lisa What do you think of ⁴ **Indiana Jones** / **James Bond** films?
Alex I love them.
Lisa I really like ⁵ **Lord of the Rings** / **Star Wars**.
Alex I think ⁶ **science fiction** / **fantasy** films are better than ⁷ **science fiction** / **fantasy** films.
Lisa I don't agree. I think they're boring!
Alex ⁸ **Action** / **Superhero** films are the best.
Lisa I agree!

4 🔘 **2.35 Look at Phrasebook. Listen and complete. Then listen again and repeat.**

5 **Work in pairs. Ask and answer questions about films. Use the ideas in Exercise 3.**

A Do you like musicals?
B No, I think they're boring.
C I agree.

Phrasebook

What films do you
¹ .... ?
Do you ² ....
action films?
I love them.
Me ³ ....
What do you
⁴ .... of
musicals?
I ⁵ .... cartoons.
I agree.
I ⁶ .... agree.

Asking for permission and offering to do things

1 🔘 **2.48** **Listen and match the conversations with the pictures.**

  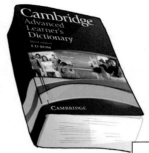 

2 🔘 **2.48** **Listen again and complete the questions. Listen once more and decide if the responses are positive (✓) or negative (✗).**

1 Could I leave the .... , please? ☒
2 Could I use your .... , please? ☐
3 Can I borrow your .... , please? ☐
4 Shall I open the .... ? ☐
5 Shall I wash the .... ? ☐
6 Shall I carry your .... ? ☐

3 🔘 **3.02** **Look at *Phrasebook*. Listen and complete the sentences. Then listen again and repeat.**

4 **Work in pairs. Act out new conversations for these situations. Take it in turns to ask for permission, offer, accept and refuse.**

PERMISSION

sit next to you
invite my friend round
play football
go out this evening

OFFERING

get a drink
turn off the radio
take out the rubbish
buy some milk

Phrasebook

Asking for permission
Can I ¹ .... your dictionary, please?
² .... I use your mobile phone, please?
Offering to do things
³ .... I open the window?
Accepting
Yes, of ⁴ ....
Sure. ⁵ .... ahead.
That's a good ⁶ ....
Thanks. That's very kind of ⁷ ....
Refusing
No, that's ⁸ ....
No, I'm ⁹ ....

Talking about the weather

1 Warm up **Look at the pictures. What's the weather like? Can you remember other words to describe the weather?**

2 ⊙ **3.12** **Listen and complete the conversations.**

Holly	What a lovely day!
Alisha	Yes, it's really hot and ¹................. .
Holly	But it's going to ²................. tomorrow.
Alisha	Oh no. Maybe we can go to the cinema.
Holly	Yes, that's a good idea.

Max	What a horrible day!
Leo	Yeah, it's so ³................. . It's really ⁴................. , too.
Max	What's the weather going to be like tomorrow?
Leo	It's going to be ⁵................. tomorrow.
Max	Great. We can go to the skate park.
Leo	Yes, let's do that.

3 ⊙ **3.13** **Look at *Phrasebook*. Listen and repeat.**

4 **Work in pairs. Act out the conversations in Exercise 2.**

5 **Work with a partner. Make notes of things you can do ...**

on a nice day	on a horrible day
go swimming	play computer games

6 **Act out your own conversations about the weather. Suggest things you can do.**

A What a lovely day!
B Yes, it's so warm.
A Maybe we can go swimming.
B Yes, let's do that.

Phrasebook

What a lovely day!
What a horrible day!
What's the weather going to be like tomorrow?
It's going to rain tomorrow.
It's going to get colder tonight.
It's going to be hot and sunny.

Working in a team

1 Warm up **Look at the picture. What do you think the friends are doing?**

Science Fact or Science Fiction?

Are these facts or are they fiction? You decide!

1 Venus is the third planet from the Sun.
2 At the top of a mountain, water boils at 100°C.
3 If you mix the colours red and blue, you make purple.
4 Leonardo da Vinci invented the bicycle.
5 The Earth is bigger than Mars.
6 The first mobile phone in 1973 weighed two kilos.
7 If you wear dark clothes on a sunny day, you will get hotter.
8 Astronauts walked on the Moon for the first time in 1979.
9 Insects have eight legs.
10 Humans need more sleep than giraffes.

2 3.22 **Listen and complete the conversation.**

Sam	OK, let's start. What's number one?
Lucy	'Venus is the third planet from the Sun.' I _____ it's true.
Sam	Are you sure?
Lucy	Erm ... well, Mercury is the first planet from the Sun. And I think Earth is the second.
Chloe	I don't agree. I'm _____ Venus is the second planet, and Earth is the third planet from the Sun.
Sam	What do you think, George?
George	I've got _____ idea!
Sam	Well, I agree with Chloe.
Lucy	Me too. Do we _____ agree?
George	Yes, OK. Venus isn't the third planet from the Sun. Let's write 'fiction'.

3 3.23 **Look at *Phrasebook*. Listen and repeat.**

4 **Work in groups of four. Act out the conversation in Exercise 2.**

5 **Work in your groups. Do the quiz.**
- Check that everyone gives an opinion. Use expressions from *Phrasebook*.
- Try to agree on your answers.
- Note your answers. Write *fact* or *fiction*.

6 **Compare your answers with other groups. Then check with your teacher.**

Phrasebook

Certain
I know this one.
I'm sure ...
Uncertain
I think ...
I'm not sure.
No idea
I've got no idea!
Checking
What do you think?
Are you sure?
Do we all agree?

10 Communication

Making compliments

1. Look at the picture. What do you think Jake is talking about? Does Emma look happy or sad?

2. 〇 3.32 Listen and complete the conversation. Then act it out.

> got   present   thanks   bag   birthday

Jake   Hi there, Emma.
Emma   Oh hi, Jake.
Jake   I like your ¹........................ .
Emma   Thanks. I ².................... it yesterday.
          It was a ³.................... from my sister.
Jake   A present?
Emma   Yeah, it was for my ⁴.................... .
Jake   Hey, I didn't know it was your birthday.
          Happy birthday, Emma!
Emma   ⁵.................... , Jake.

3. 〇 3.33 Listen and match the exchanges.

1 Hey, Jake. What a cool jumper!   A Thanks. I downloaded it yesterday.
2 Your mp3 player is really nice.   B Do you think so? Thanks. I practise a lot.
3 I like your skateboard.   C Thanks. It's new.
4 What an amazing ringtone!   D Thanks. I bought it on Saturday.
5 I think your singing is really good. E Do you think so? Thanks. I got it last week.

4. 〇 3.34 Look at *Phrasebook*. Listen and repeat.

5. Take it in turns to make compliments to each other. Choose from the following ideas. Use different expressions from *Phrasebook*.

> English   new bike   jeans   handwriting   T-shirt
> hair   mobile   cat   dancing   rucksack

A Hey, Anna. Your English is really good.
B Thanks. I do a lot of homework!

6. Make real compliments to your partner. You can talk about his/her clothes, books, bags … anything!

Student A
Make a compliment.

Student B
Say 'Thanks' and add some information.

Make a compliment.

Say 'Thanks' and add some information.

Phrasebook

Making compliments
I like your bag.
I love your mobile.
Your bike is really cool!
What a fantastic hat!
Accepting compliments
Thanks! It was a present.
Do you think so? Thanks.
I got it last year.

 WB page 81   Communication   **Unit 10**   **117**

Irregular verbs

Verb	Past simple	Past participle
be	was/were	been
beat	beat	beaten
become	became	become
begin	began	begun
bite	bit	bitten
break	broke	broken
bring	brought	brought
build	built	built
buy	bought	bought
catch	caught	caught
choose	chose	chosen
come	came	come
cost	cost	cost
cut	cut	cut
do	did	done
drink	drank	drunk
drive	drove	driven
eat	ate	eaten
fall	fell	fallen
feel	felt	felt
fight	fought	fought
find	found	found
fly	flew	flown
forget	forgot	forgotten
get	got	got
give	gave	given
go	went	gone
grow	grew	grown
hang	hung	hung
have	had	had
hear	heard	heard
hit	hit	hit
hold	held	held
keep	kept	kept
know	knew	known

Verb	Past simple	Past participle
leave	left	left
lose	lost	lost
make	made	made
meet	met	met
pay	paid	paid
put	put	put
read	read	read
ride	rode	ridden
ring	rang	rung
run	ran	run
say	said	said
see	saw	seen
sell	sold	sold
send	sent	sent
shake	shook	shaken
sing	sang	sung
sink	sank	sunk
sit	sat	sat
sleep	slept	slept
speak	spoke	spoken
spend	spent	spent
stand	stood	stood
steal	stole	stolen
swim	swam	swum
take	took	taken
teach	taught	taught
tell	told	told
think	thought	thought
understand	understood	understood
upset	upset	upset
wake	woke	woken
wear	wore	worn
win	won	won
write	wrote	written

The Old House

by Martyn Hobbs

Contents

Episode 1 ⦿ 3.35

The RUNNING MAN

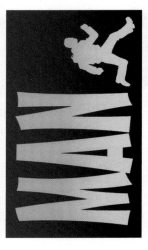

Episode 2 ◉ 3.36
A Family Legend

Episode 3 ● 3.37

Great Great
Aunt Mabel's
House

On Saturday morning, Ruby and Ben go for a bike ride.

HEY, STOP A MINUTE!

THERE WAS A ROBBERY FROM A SHOP NEAR HERE YESTERDAY. THAT'S SCARY.

WHEN DID IT HAPPEN?

SOME TIME IN THE AFTERNOON. THEY THINK A MAN DID IT.

THIEF STEALS THOUSANDS OF POUNDS

DID HE TAKE A LOT OF MONEY?

YES, HE DID. HEY, BEN, DO YOU THINK IT WAS THE GUY IN THE STREET?

NO, I DON'T. COME ON!

They soon arrive at their destination.

SO THIS IS IT – GREAT GREAT AUNT MABEL'S HOUSE!

WHEN DID SHE LIVE HERE?

OH, ABOUT 50 YEARS AGO, I THINK.

MAYBE SHE HID HER MONEY IN THE GARDEN.

DAD HAS AN OLD METAL DETECTOR IN THE GARAGE. WE CAN USE THAT!

Ruby suddenly looks up at the house.

WHAT'S UP?

I THOUGHT I HEARD A NOISE.

DON'T BE SILLY. THE HOUSE IS EMPTY. NOBODY'S LIVING THERE!

Episode 4 · 3.38

The Metal Detector

1. On Sunday afternoon, Ruby and Ben explore the garage.

Maybe it's under here... Yes, here it is!

It's the oldest metal detector in the world! We can't use that. It's too embarrassing!

2. Half an hour later...

It's a lot colder than yesterday.

Stop complaining! This is the most exciting thing ever!

3. OK, you look in the flower beds. I want to explore by the pond.

Can I use the metal detector?

No, you can't. I carried it here, so it's my turn first.

4. We've got cans, plastic bags... The most valuable thing is this old spoon! The garden's just full of rubbish.

Listen, Ben. There's something big under here. Maybe it's great great Aunt Mabel's metal box!

5. Ben starts digging... But it's hard work!

Dig deeper, Ben.

Why didn't we bring a bigger spade? Wait. I think I can see it! What is it?

6. Erm... It's a saucepan. And it's got a hole in it.

Ruby, it's cold, it's dark, and I'm hungry.

OK, OK. But I'd really like to come back. There's still lots to explore!

Episode 5 ● 3.39

The SHAPE in the WINDOW

1 RUBY IS IN THE SCHOOL CANTEEN... BUT SHE ISN'T THINKING ABOUT HER LUNCH.

WHAT ARE YOU LOOKING AT?

OH, IT'S JUST SOMETHING I FILMED THE OTHER DAY.

2 RUBY SHOWS HER MOBILE PHONE TO HER FRIEND ZARA.

TELL ME WHAT YOU CAN SEE.

IT ISN'T VERY CLEAR. THERE'S ERM... A BROKEN WINDOW...

3 YES, BUT LOOK. THERE'S A SHAPE. CAN YOU SEE IT? AND IT'S MOVING!

SO WHAT? THERE'S A PERSON IN THE ROOM.

BUT THAT'S IMPOSSIBLE. THE HOUSE IS EMPTY.

REALLY? THEN MAYBE IT'S A GHOST!

I DON'T BELIEVE IN GHOSTS.

OR... HEE!

4 DIDN'T YOU HEAR THE BELL? IT'S TIME FOR YOUR NEXT LESSON.

OH, YES. SORRY, MR SMITH. COME ON, ZARA!

5 AFTER SCHOOL, RUBY TELLS BEN ABOUT THE GHOST. THEN ZARA MAKES A SUGGESTION.

WHAT ARE YOU DOING ON SATURDAY?

I DON'T KNOW.

WE'RE GOING ICE-SKATING. DO YOU WANT TO COME?

WE'D LOVE TO, BUT WE'RE BUSY.

6 WHAT DO YOU MEAN, WE'RE BUSY? I LIKE ICE-SKATING!

WE'RE GOING BACK TO THE HOUSE. I THINK THE METAL BOX IS INSIDE.

OH, BEN! MAYBE IT'S GREAT GREAT AUNT MABEL'S GHOST! SHE WANTS TO SHOW US HER SECRET BOX!

WHAT ABOUT THE GHOST?

Episode 6 ● 3.40
An Amazing Discovery

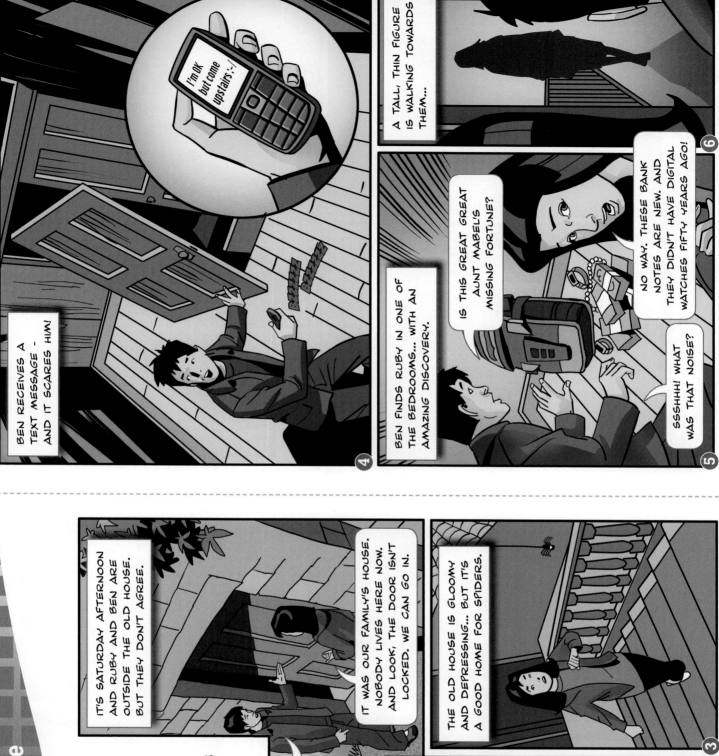

1. IT'S SATURDAY AFTERNOON AND RUBY AND BEN ARE OUTSIDE THE OLD HOUSE. BUT THEY DON'T AGREE.

THIS ISN'T A GOOD IDEA. IT ISN'T OUR HOUSE.

IT WAS OUR FAMILY'S HOUSE. NOBODY LIVES HERE NOW. AND LOOK, THE DOOR ISN'T LOCKED. WE CAN GO IN.

3. THE OLD HOUSE IS GLOOMY AND DEPRESSING... BUT IT'S A GOOD HOME FOR SPIDERS.

2. OK, YOU LOOK DOWN HERE. I CAN SEARCH UPSTAIRS.

WHY DO I HAVE TO LOOK ON MY OWN?

BECAUSE IT'S QUICKER. WE CAN KEEP IN TOUCH WITH TEXT MESSAGES. WE MUST BE QUIET, BEN.

4. BEN RECEIVES A TEXT MESSAGE - AND IT SCARES HIM!

I'm OK but come upstairs :-|

5. BEN FINDS RUBY IN ONE OF THE BEDROOMS... WITH AN AMAZING DISCOVERY.

IS THIS GREAT GREAT AUNT MABEL'S MISSING FORTUNE?

NO WAY. THESE BANK NOTES ARE NEW. AND THEY DIDN'T HAVE DIGITAL WATCHES FIFTY YEARS AGO!

SSSHHH! WHAT WAS THAT NOISE?

6. A TALL, THIN FIGURE IS WALKING TOWARDS THEM...

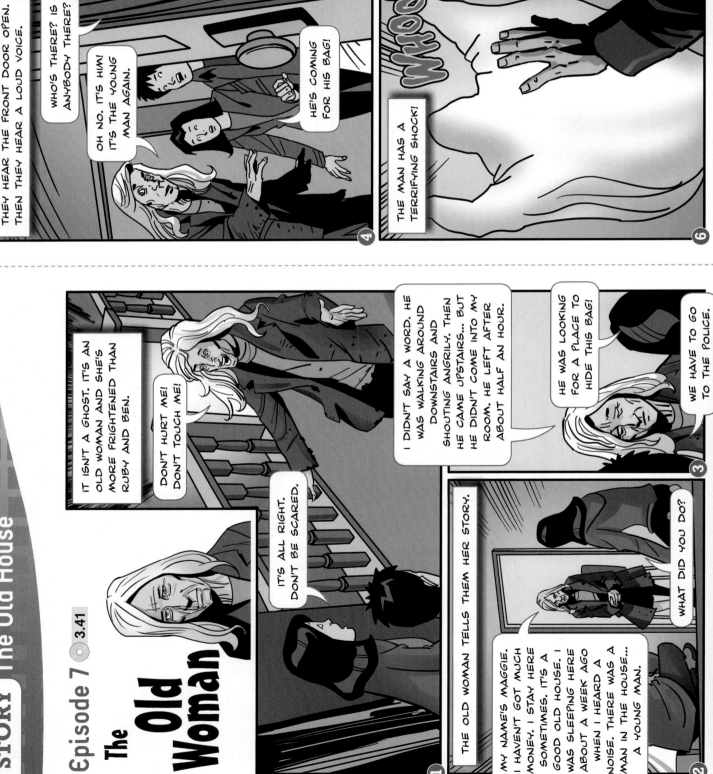

Episode 8 ⊙ 3.42
Great Great Aunt Mabel's Gift

1 BEN HAS A BIG SURPRISE.

WELL DONE, BEN! YOU WERE A BRILLIANT GHOST.

I DON'T BELIEVE IT, RUBY! HE'S THE GUY I SAW IN THE STREET!

AARRGH...

RUBY TELLS THE POLICE OFFICER ABOUT THEIR RELATIVE AND HER SECRET BOX.

THAT'S VERY INTERESTING, RUBY. BUT THEY'RE GOING TO KNOCK DOWN THIS OLD HOUSE SOON. THEY'RE PLANNING TO BUILD SOME NEW FLATS HERE.

OH NO!

BUT YOU CAN EXPLORE THE GARDEN NEXT WEEKEND.

2 RUBY PHONES THE POLICE... AND FIVE MINUTES LATER THEY ARREST THE MAN.

YOU KNOW, THERE'S A £1,000 REWARD FOR ALL THIS. YOU KIDS ARE GOING TO GET A LOT OF MONEY.

NO, WE AREN'T. MAGGIE'S GOING TO GET THE REWARD.

WHAT? OH YEAH. OF COURSE.

THAT'S VERY KIND OF YOU.

4 ONE WEEK LATER THEY RETURN TO THE GARDEN. THIS TIME BEN HAS GOT A BIGGER SPADE!

HEY, BEN! COME OVER HERE AND START DIGGING.

WAIT FOR ME, DAD!

EEEEEEEE!

5 BEN LIFTS A METAL BOX OUT OF THE GROUND... AND RUBY OPENS IT.

WELL, RUBY? DID GREAT GREAT AUNT MABEL LEAVE ALL HER MONEY IN THERE?

NO, SHE DIDN'T. BUT SHE GAVE US A FANTASTIC GIFT.

WHAT IS IT?

6 THESE ARE HER DIARIES. THEY'RE THE STORY OF HER LIFE!

ARE THEY AS GOOD AS MONEY?

THEY'RE BETTER THAN THAT! AND I'M GOING TO PUT THEM ALL IN MY PROJECT!

Unit 1

1 (Circle) the correct answer.
1 There are too **much / many** people.
2 You don't eat **enough / many** fruit.
3 I've got **enough / too many** things.
4 My sister gives our dog too **much / many** food.
5 Six cats! You've got too **much / many**!
6 Oh dear. There aren't **much / enough** chairs in this room.

2 (Circle) the correct answer.
1 I often .... to the cinema on Friday.
   a am going **b** (go) **c** goes
2 Hi! What are you .... ?
   a does **b** do **c** doing
3 What time do you .... breakfast?
   a has **b** have **c** having
4 It's six o'clock. My dad .... home from work.
   a drives **b** is driving **c** drive
5 I .... hip hop music.
   a 'm liking **b** like **c** likes
6 I usually cycle to school but this week I .... the bus.
   a get **b** 'm getting **c** getting
7 Tom .... the guitar very well.
   a can plays **b** can play **c** can playing
8 Carrie .... her red jacket today.
   a wears **b** is wearing **c** does wear
9 Paolo and Enrico aren't at home now. They .... football.
   a is playing **b** are playing **c** play
10 It .... a lot in the winter here.
   a is snowing **b** snow **c** snows

3 ◉ 1.12 **Listen and complete the text.**
It's Monday morning and we're on holiday! So what's different? Well, Mum ¹ *is reading* a book in the garden. She usually ² .... in an office on Monday. Dad is a teacher. He ³ .... French at my school, but today he' ⁴ .... rock music on his guitar! My brother Mattia is a university student and he usually ⁵ .... at the library in the morning. But today he' ⁶ .... computer games. My sister, Giorgia, is a cook in a restaurant. But she ⁷ .... at the moment, she' ⁸ .... a romantic film on TV. And I usually ⁹ .... Science on Monday morning. But today I' ¹⁰ .... my blog. I love holidays!

Unit 2

1 **Complete the sentences with the past simple form of the verb *be*. Use the positive (✓), negative (✗) or question (?) form.**
1 It __was__ a lovely day yesterday. (✓)
2 .... you at school last week (?)
3 There .... any lions at the zoo. (✗)
4 I .... really tired last night. (✓)
5 Where .... Dan and Anna (?)
6 Monet .... a great artist. (✓)
7 .... I a good baby (?)
8 My brother .... at football practice last night. (✓)

2 **Complete the sentences with the past simple form of these verbs.**

go   watch   win   give   ride   text   cook
wear   visit   ~~walk~~

1 I __walked__ to school yesterday because my bike had a flat tyre.
2 Last week I .... a fantastic science museum in London.
3 We .... a curry last night.
4 Meg .... a volleyball match yesterday.
5 My sister .... her boyfriend ten times last night!
6 I .... my new T-shirt to the party.
7 She .... a horse on Saturday.
8 My teacher .... to Lapland for Christmas.
9 Vicky .... first prize in an art competition.
10 Look at my camera. My parents ....it to me for my birthday!

3 ◉ 1.29 **Listen and complete the text.**
We ¹ *went* to Paris on holiday last year. We ² .... in a lovely flat. There was a fantastic view of the city. There ³ .... three big bedrooms and a living room. We ⁴ .... to all the museums and visited the sights. We walked a lot and ⁵ .... by bus. We ⁶ .... a boat ride on the River Seine and climbed the Eiffel Tower. We ⁷ .... French coffee in the morning, and we ⁸ .... in restaurants in the evening. I really ⁹ .... my holiday and I ¹⁰ .... a blog about it.

Unit 3

1 Write negative sentences in the past simple.

1 I / not watch / a tennis match
I didn't watch a tennis match.
2 Isabel and James / not go / to school
3 We / not like / those pizzas
4 They / not sing / in the show
5 She / not spend / any money
6 You / not call / me last night

2 Complete the questions and answers with the correct form of the past simple.

1 Did you enjoy your weekend? (enjoy)
Yes, I did .
2 _____ your mum _____ you? (help)
No, she _____ .
3 _____ they _____ to school yesterday? (walk)
Yes, they _____ .
4 _____ David _____ computer games last night? (play)
No, he _____ .
5 _____ you run fast when you were a child? (can)
No, I _____ .
6 What _____ you _____ for breakfast this morning? (have)
I _____ cereal and milk. (have)
7 Who _____ you _____ at the party? (see)
I _____ Chloe. (see)
8 Where _____ you _____ for your holiday? (go)
We _____ to Portugal. (go)

3 ◎ **1.41 Listen and complete the text.**

Last Friday we [1] didn't have lessons. What did we [2] _____ ? We visited a zoo and then we [3] _____ to a theme park. We [4] _____ a long time at the zoo. We saw some brilliant animals. My best friend, Dan, [5] _____ the snakes but I [6] _____ them! At the theme park there were some fantastic rides. I liked the ghost train, but Dan [7] _____ on it. He was scared! At lunchtime we [8] _____ in the restaurant. We sat outside and [9] _____ sandwiches and ice cream. It was perfect. And we [10] _____ any homework because it was a school trip!

Unit 4

1 Circle the correct answer.

1 My dog is _____ than your cat!
a intelligent   b most intelligent
c more intelligent
2 Today isn't very hot. Yesterday was
_____ .
a hottest   b hotter   c more hot
3 That actor isn't very good looking.
This actor is _____ .
a best looking   b better looking
c better
4 I'm 13. Tom's 13, too. Tom is _____ me.
a as old as   b older than   c the oldest
5 My school bag isn't very heavy. Your bag
is _____ .
a heavier   b more heavy   c heaviest
6 This computer isn't very fast. My dad's
is _____ .
a fastest   b the fast   c faster

2 Complete the sentences with the superlative form of the adjectives in brackets.

1 The heaviest animal is the blue whale. It weighs 190,000 kilos! (heavy)
2 Robert Wadlow, the _____ man, was 2.72 metres tall. (tall)
3 The _____ land animal is the cheetah. (fast)
4 Barack Obama is probably the _____ politician. (famous)
5 The _____ car is the Bugatti Veyron. It costs $1,700,000! (expensive)
6 The _____ bicycle is over 28 metres long! (long)

3 ◎ **2.08 Listen and complete the text.**

Our new house

We moved here last week and I love it. It's [1] bigger than our old house. And it's [2] _____ . My bedroom is smaller but it's [3] _____ . There's a really big window and I've got a great view. The living room is [4] _____ before, but the kitchen is larger. The garden is [5] _____ too. There's a pond and lots of trees. The shops near my house are [6] _____ than the shops near my old house. The local park is [7] _____ – there's a skate park. It's not as [8] _____ to my school [9] _____ our old house, but the journey is [10] _____ on the bus!

Unit 5

1 **Complete the conversation with the correct form of the present continuous.**

Sarah Hi, how are you?

Abbie I'm fine. What [1] _are_ you _doing_ at the weekend? (do)

Sarah I [2] _____ (go) round to my cousin's house. I [3] _____ (stay) the night. What about you?

Abbie I [4] _____ (play) in a hockey match tomorrow. My team [5] _____ (go) there by bus.

Sarah Cool. [6] _____ Eve and Anna (go) too?

Abbie No, they [7] _____ . They [8] _____ (play) tomorrow.

Sarah Right. Well, good luck! What about Sunday? [9] _____ you (come) to the swimming pool?

Abbie Yes, I [10] _____ . See you there.

2 **Look at Mark's diary and write sentences with the present continuous or may.**

Mark may watch a film on Monday.
Mark is doing karate at 6 pm.

✓ = sure	? = not sure
Monday watch a film **?**	**Friday** do my Maths project **?**
Tuesday do karate 6 pm ✓	**Saturday** buy a new computer game ✓
Wednesday practise the guitar **?**	**Sunday** go to see my grandparents **?**
Thursday tidy my bedroom ✓	

3 **2.19 Listen and complete the text.**

We've got a busy weekend. Tonight we're [1] _going_ to the supermarket. Then on Saturday it's my brother's sixteenth birthday. He's [2] _____ to London for the day with some friends. They're [3] _____ the Science Museum. I [4] _____ go with them, but I'm not sure. I [5] _____ go skateboarding with my friends. Then in the evening we're all [6] _____ a Mexican meal. On Sunday my aunt and uncle [7] _____ visiting. We're [8] _____ a big Sunday lunch and my mum's [9] _____ a cake! After lunch my uncle [10] _____ take us out in his sports car!

Unit 6

1 **Complete the sentences with should or shouldn't.**

1 It's late! You _should_ go to bed.

2 She really wants to go to the concert so she _____ buy a ticket quickly.

3 That's dangerous! You _____ try that at home.

4 I'm not very fit. I _____ do more exercise.

5 My parents are very angry with me! You _____ copy other students in tests.

6 Those jeans are too expensive. You _____ buy them.

7 She's not very good at speaking English. She _____ practise more.

8 That's naughty! You _____ do that.

2 **Circle the correct answer.**

| **Packing for a holiday** |

Ben Mum, [1] **do I must / do I have to** take a sweater?

Mum Yes, you do. You [2] **should / don't have to** take the blue one. And you [3] **shouldn't / should** pack these sandals.

Ben Oh, Mum! I hate sandals.

Mum Oh, Ben! And your sister is packing too many clothes. Grace, you [4] **don't have to / must** pack all the clothes in your wardrobe! Pack your books, too. You [5] **have to / shouldn't** do some homework on holiday.

Grace But, Mum, I [6] **don't have to / mustn't** study this week!

Mum OK. You can have one week's break.

3 **2.31 Listen and complete the text.**

You [1] _should get_ the number 10 bus. You [2] _____ at the bus stop at the end of my road. You [3] _____ your ticket from a shop, you have [4] _____ it from the bus driver. Remember to tell [5] _____ that you are under 16, because the ticket is cheaper. [6] _____ a return ticket to the city centre – it costs £1.50. [7] _____ takes about 20 minutes. [8] _____ at the Town Hall.

Unit 7

1 Rewrite the sentences using an adverb.

1 Jake's a good guitar player.
   He plays the guitar very well.
2 She's a dangerous driver.
3 You're a fast walker.
4 Oscar is a bad player.
5 I'm a slow swimmer.
6 We're careful cyclists.

2 Circle the correct answer.

1 She **was working** / **worked** when I was **phoning** / **phoned** her.
2 We **were playing** / **played** football when it **was starting** / **started** to rain.
3 The phone **was ringing** / **rang** when I **was listening** / **listened** to music.
4 We **were seeing** / **saw** the famous singer when he **was getting** / **got** out of his limousine.
5 Paul and I **were waiting** / **waited** at the bus stop when we **were seeing** / **saw** the accident.
6 We **were cooking** / **cooked** dinner when the dog **was stealing** / **stole** the meat.
7 I **was studying** / **studied** when you **were sending** / **sent** me that text message.
8 My brother **was having** / **had** breakfast when I **was leaving** / **left** the house.

3 ◎ **2.45 Listen and complete the text.**

I ¹ *had* an accident last week. I ² _____ for school and we had a Maths test. It ³ _____ and the roads were wet. I ⁴ _____ very fast down a hill when a cat ran into the road. I tried to stop. I ⁵ _____ the cat but I fell off my bike. Luckily I was wearing my helmet so I ⁶ _____ hurt my head. But I really hurt my arm. I ⁷ _____ on the ground when a car ⁸ _____ . It was my friend's mum. She ⁹ _____ me to the hospital and the doctor checked my arm. It was OK but I ¹⁰ _____ with it. So I didn't do my Maths test!

Unit 8

1 Write questions using the prompts. Then match them to the answers.

1 where / you / work ?
   Where are you going to work?
   At my desk
2 what / you / do after lunch?
3 who / you / phone?
4 when / you / tidy your room?
5 which film / you / watch?
6 what / you / eat for dinner?

a Tomorrow!
b *Spiderman*.
c At my desk.
d Sophia.
e Play football with George.
f A chicken salad.

2 Complete the sentences with the correct form of *be going to*.

1 I *'m going to learn* to play the piano. (learn)
2 Jessica _____ a party on Saturday night. (have)
3 Steve _____ at home tonight. (not eat)
4 I _____ a ticket for the pop festival. (buy)
5 _____ you the new James Bond film? (see)
6 Oh no! I think it _____ . (rain)

3 ◎ **3.10 Listen and complete the text.**

My friends and I have a lot of plans for this summer. We're ¹ *going to* go to England and study English. We're going to ² _____ in Brighton with English families. We're ³ _____ all the sights in London and we're going to ⁴ _____ lots of souvenirs! I'm going to ⁵ _____ lots of photos. When we get back, I'm going to ⁶ _____ a blog about England and ⁷ _____ going to put my photos on it. My friend Riccardo is going to ⁸ _____ . And my friend Holly is going to do a lot of ⁹ _____ . But we ¹⁰ _____ going to do any school work!

Unit 9

1 Read Paola's and Juan's New Year predictions. Write four sentences about each of them. Use *will* or *might*.

Paola will learn to skateboard.
Paola might learn to play the piano.

NEXT YEAR'S PREDICTIONS

Paola

Sure	Not sure
learn to skateboard	learn to play the piano
go to London	go to Edinburgh
buy a new computer	buy a pet

Juan

Sure	Not sure
play football a lot	play in the school team
swim in the sea	learn to dive

2 Circle the correct form of the verbs.

1 If I **don't see** / **won't see** Jamie at school, I'll call him on my mobile.
2 I **download** / **'ll download** this song if you like it.
3 You'll miss the bus if you **don't leave** / **won't leave** soon.
4 Will you send me an email if I **give** / **'ll give** you my email address?
5 If Lucy **doesn't get** / **won't get** a ticket, she won't go to the concert.
6 Will the dog run after the ball if I **throw** / **'ll throw** it?
7 If I **leave** / **'ll leave** now, I'll see my friends.
8 I **see** / **'ll see** you on Sunday if I have time.

3 ◯ **3.20** Listen and complete the text.

My future life *by Jodie*

If I pass all my exams I'll [1] .... to university. I might study Science or languages, I'm not sure. I [2] .... stay in my city so I can be with my friends, or I [3] .... go to another city. After university [4] .... travel around the world for a year with my friends. [5] .... have fun. We'll visit lots of interesting places and meet people. I [6] .... do some work with poor people, or I [7] .... work with animals. After I get home, I'll [8] .... to become a teacher. I [9] .... teach little children because I love them! But it's difficult to be sure about the future. I [10] .... become a famous singer or an actor!

Unit 10

1 Write the past participles of these verbs.

1 buy ....
2 sleep ....
3 give ....
4 eat ....
5 meet ....
6 hear ....
7 read ....
8 come ....
9 write ....
10 speak ....

2 Circle the correct answer.

1 .... you ever swum in the sea?
  a Have **b** Has
2 I haven't .... to France. I would like to.
  a be **b** been
3 My parents .... me a new bike.
  a have bought **b** has bought
4 Has your sister .... that book?
  a reading **b** read
5 I .... yoga. Is it fun?
  a haven't done **b** hasn't done
6 We've .... this game before. Is it good?
  a ever played **b** never played
7 Has your teacher .... visited America?
  a ever **b** never
8 .... a new school. It's nice.
  a I've started **b** I start
9 We .... downloaded a film.
  a haven't **b** didn't
10 Has she seen the film? Yes, she ....
  a did **b** has

3 ◯ **3.30** Listen and complete the text.

An amazing life

Luke has travelled all over the world. He's [1] .... diving in Australia and he's [2] .... mountains in Switzerland. He's [3] .... marathons in London and New York, and he's raised lots of money for charity. He's [4] .... in an old car all over Europe, and he's [5] .... in a boat around the world. He's [6] .... to the Antarctic and studied polar bears. And he's [7] .... a lot of famous people too. But Luke doesn't like modern life very much. He [8] .... never [9] .... an email. And he's got a mobile phone but he's never [10] .... a text message. So if you want to contact him, send him a letter!

Your Space

Web Zone

http://yourspace.cambridge.org

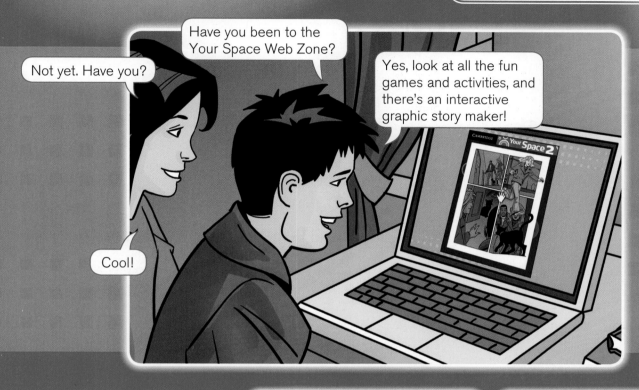

Your Space

DVD

Featuring:

Video diaries

Viewpoints

Communication

Culture

CLIL

Surprise your teens!

These fabulous activities are
sure to get them involved.
Just photocopy and go!

Thanks and Acknowledgements

The authors and publishers would like to thank the teachers who commented on the material at different stages of its development, the teachers who allowed us to observe their classes, and those who gave up their valuable time for interviews and focus groups. Unfortunately, space does not allow us to mention these people individually by name.

The authors would like to thank all the people who have worked so hard on Your Space. We are especially grateful to James Dingle for inviting us to write this project and for his support during all stages of its development. We would also like to thank Frances Amrani, commissioning editor, and the editors Claire Powell, Rosemary Bradley and Ruth Bell-Pellegrini for their skilled editorial contributions, perceptive editing, and commitment to the project; the design team at Wild Apple; David Lawton for his design ideas; Emma Szlachta for her excellent project management and Graham Avery, production manager for his support. We are grateful to all the other writers on the project for their creative input. We would also like to thank the many reviewers and teachers who contributed to the development of this course. We extend a special thank you to the publisher Rachael Gibbon for her unwavering focus during the development process.

The publishers acknowledge the following sources of copyright material and are grateful for the permissions granted. While every effort has been made, it has not always been possible to identify the sources of all the material used, or to trace all copyright holders. If any omissions are brought to our notice, we will be happy to include the appropriate acknowledgements on reprinting.

Photo Acknowledgements

p. 9 (T): Shutterstock/Andry Shadrin; p. 9 (B): Shutterstock/AVAVA; p. 10: Shutterstock/Dmitriy Shironosov; p. 17 (L): © Radius Images / Alamy; p. 17 (R): © Beyond Fotomedia GmbH / Alamy; p. 18 (photo 1): Shutterstock/Agb; p. 18 (photo 2): Shutterstock/olly; p. 18 (photo 3): Shutterstock/Valery Bareta; p. 18 (photo 4 & 6): Shutterstock/Bartlomiej Nowak; p. 18 (photo 5): Shutterstock/Olaru Radian-Alexandru; p. 18 (photo 7): Shutterstock/Mikael Damkier; p. 18 (photo 8): Shutterstock/Ivan Kruk; p. 18 (photo 9): Shutterstock/Christopher Sykes; p. 18 (photo 10): Shutterstock//lush; p. 25: Shutterstock/Pichugin Dimitry; p. 27 (TC): Shutterstock/roseburn; p. 27 (CL): © Sergio Pitamitz / Alamy; p. 27 (TR): © John Warburton-Lee/JAI/Corbis; p. 27 (BR): Shutterstock/EcoPrint; p. 29 (L): imagebroker / Alamy; p. 29 (R): Andrew Price/Rex Features; p. 31: Shutterstock/Tyler Olsen; p. 34 (CL): Thinkstock/Ryan McVay; p. 34 (CR): Thinkstock; p. 34 (TR): Shutterstock/Yarek Gora; p. 35: Shutterstock/Lisa F. Young; p. 37 (L & C): Getty Images; p. 37 (R): Science and Society/Superstock; p. 44 (L): © Stephen Frink Collection / Alamy; p. 44 (R): Chris Bjornberg / Science Photo Library; p. 44 (C): © David Tipling / Alamy; p. 46 (photo 1): Shutterstock/Wendy Kaveney Photography; p. 46 (photo 2): Shutterstock/Lori Skelton; p. 46 (photo 3): Shutterstock/Viorel Sima; p. 46 (photo 4): Shutterstock/Robin Jr.; p. 46 (photo 5): Frans Lanting/FLPA; p. 46 (photo 6): Shutterstock/Susan Quinland-Stringer; p. 46 (photo 7): Shutterstock/Mayskyphoto; p. 46 (photo 8): Shutterstock/Eric Issel e; p. 46 (photo 9): Shutterstock/Pavel Reband; p. 46 (photo 10): Shutterstock/Selyutina Olga; p. 47 (photo a): Alamy/Niall McDiarmid; p. 47 (b): Ruth Bell-Pellegrini; p. 47 (c): Thinkstock; p. 47 (photo d): Shutterstock/ronstik; p. 48 (TL): Shutterstock/Brett Mulcahy; p. 48 (TC): Shutterstock/Jose Gil; p. 48 (TR): © Francesco Survara / Alamy; p. 48 (BL): Shutterstock/bhowe; p. 48 (BC): Shutterstock/sokolovsky; p. 48 (BR): Shutterstock/Kheng Guan Toh; p. 51 (TL, TC, CR, CL & BL): Thinkstock; p. 51 (TR): Shutterstock/Martin Allinger; p. 51 (C): Dreamstime/© Sebcz; p. 51 (BC): Alamy/Chris Cooper-Smith; p. 51 (BR): Alamy/Paul Fleet; p. 53 (TL): Pictures Colour Library/Brian Lawrence Images Ltd; p. 53 (TR): © MBI / Alamy; p. 53 (Theo): Shutterstock/Galina Barskaya; p. 53 (Naomi): Shutterstock/JJ Pix; p. 53 (Harvey): Shutterstock/Monkey Business Images; p. 53 (Alisha): © Dennis MacDonald / Alamy; p. 53 (Brandon): Shutterstock/Yuri Arcurs; p. 53 (Caitlin): Shutterstock/Elena Elisseeva; p. 56T (B/G): Kwame Zikomo/Purestock/Superstock; p. 56 (CL): Nils Jorgensen/Rex Features; p. 56 (BL): © Richard Klune/Corbis; p. 56 (CR): Lemur Leisure Ltd; p. 56 (BR): Neale Haynes/Rex Features; p. 72 (TL): © Stan Kujawa / Alamy; p. 72 (TCL): Shutterstock/zimmytws; p. 72 (TCR): Shutterstock/Craig Barhorst; p. 72 (TR): © avatra images / Alamy; p. 72 (BL): INSADCO Photography/Photolibrary Group; p. 72 (BCL): © Qrt / Alamy; p. 72 (BCR): © Steve Lindridge / Alamy; p. 72 (BR): Shutterstock/svehlik; p. 74: Photodisc; p. 78 (photo 1): Shutterstock/Alexander Raths; p. 78 (photo 2): Shutterstock/Monkey Business Images; p. 78 (photo 3): © imagebroker / Alamy; p. 78 (photo 4): Shutterstock/Chad McDermott; p. 78 (photo 5): Shutterstock/visi stock; p. 78 (photo 6): Miramax/Imagine/Parkway Productions / The Kobal Collection; p. 78 (photo 7): Shutterstock/Schmid Christophe; p. 78 (photo 8): Shutterstock/T-Design; p. 78 (photo 9): Shutterstock/Rob Marmion; p. 78 (photo 10): © Horizon International Images Limited / Alamy; p. 78 (photo 11): © Stan Fellerman/Corbis; p. 78 (photo 12): © GabiGarcia / Alamy; p. 79 (TR B/G): Francisco Cruz/Purestock/Superstock; p. 79 (TL & TC B/G): Lisette Le Bon/Purestock/Superstock; p. 79 (inset): Shutterstock/christo; p. 81 (TL): Thinkstock; p. 81 (TC): Thinkstock/ Jupiterimages; p. 81 (TR): Thinkstock/Jack Hollingsworth; p. 81 (BL): Thinkstock/Ryan McVay; p. 81 (BR): Thinkstock/Photodisc; p. 86: Photofusion/© David Trainer; p. 90: Shutterstock/Eduard Stelmakh; p. 91: Shutterstock/AND Inc.; p. 95 (UCL): Shutterstock/Yellowj; p. 95 (UCR): Shutterstock/Susan McKenzie; p. 96 (TR): LucasFilm/20th Century Fox / The Kobal Collection; p. 96 (UCL): 20th Century Fox / The Kobal Collection / Digital Domain; p. 96 (BCL): c.BuenaVist/Everett/Rex Features; p. 96 (BL): Amblin/Dreamworks/WB / The Kobal Collection / James, David; p. 96 (TL): NASA/Science Photo Library; p. 101: Thinkstock/Karl Weatherly; p. 102 (L): Thinkstock; p. 102 (R): Science Photo Library/Gemini Observatory / NOAO / AURA / NSF; p. 103 (CR): © Vincent Ball / Alamy; p. 103 (CL): Alamy/Niall McDiarmid; p. 103 (BL): Getty Images/Mike Marsland/WireImage; p. 103 (BR): Thinkstock; p. 106 (TR): Rex Features/Tom Dymond; p. 106 (BL): Getty Images/Vladimir Rys; p. 106 (BR): Getty Images/Philip Brown; p. 107 (L): Getty Images/Bryn Lennon; p. 107 (R): Thinkstock; p. 111: © The Natural History Museum, London.

We are unable to locate the copyright holder of the photograph on p. 47 (B/G) and would appreciate any information which would enable us to do so.

Commissioned photography by Gareth Boden/Cambridge University Press for pages 13, 19, 33, 39, 49, 59, 69, 83, 89, 93, 99, 103 (TR)

Artwork Acknowledgements

Jake Lawrence pp. 10, 11, 14 (L), 20 (T), 30, 40, 44, 50, 54, 60, 64 (L), 70 (T), 74 (T), 80, 84 (T), 90, 94 (L), 100; David Benham p. 12, 26, 41 (R), 55 (L), 64 (R), 97; Humberto Blanco p. 14 (R), p22, 42, 70 (B), 85 (L); Ned Woodman p. 15, 25, 35, 45, 55 (R), 65, 75 (R), 85 (R), 105; Simon Rumble p16, 32, 62; Pete Smith p. 20 (B), p23, 61, 75 (L), 94 (R); Andy Parker p. 21, 89; Adrian Barclay p. 28, 38, 52, 82, 84 (L); Laszlo Veres p. 36; Matt Ward p. 41, 84 (R), 92; Mike Lacey p. 50, 101; Jo Taylor p. 68, 73; Kevin Hopgood p. 71, 119-127, 133; Andrew Hennessey p. 74, 98; Emmanuel Cerisier p. 76, 77, 104; Martin Bustamante p. 88; Carl Pearce pp. 108-117

The publishers would like to extend a warm thanks to all the teachers and freelance collaborators who have made a valuable contribution to this material.